M

AN AMERICAN POSTCARD COLLECTOR'S GUIDE

AN AMERICAN POSTCARD COLLECTOR'S GUIDE

Valerie Monahan

BLANDFORD PRESS
POOLE   DORSET

First published in the U.K. 1981 by Blandford Press,
Link House, West Street, Poole, Dorset, BH15 1LL

British Library Cataloguing in Publication Data

Monahan, Valerie
  An American Postcard Collector's Guide
  1. Postal cards — Collectors and Collecting —
  United States
  I. Title
  769.5   NC1872

ISBN 0 7137 1113 2

Phototypeset by Oliver Burridge & Co. Ltd, Crawley, Sussex
Printed in Great Britain by Tonbridge Printers Ltd, Tonbridge, Kent

CONTENTS

ACKNOWLEDGEMENTS

My thanks are due to Sally S. Carver, the author of *The American Postcard Guide to Tuck,* and to Jocelyn D. Decker, Secretary of the Webfooter Postcard Club, Portland, Oregon, for their help and encouragement, especially during the preparation of the section concerned with the valuations of American postcards; to Barbara Andrews, the compiler of *A Directory of Postcards, Artists, Publishers and Trademarks,* and to George and Dorothy Miller, the authors of *Picture Postcards in the United States 1893–1918*—both books I found to be quite indispensable when it came to checking essential dates and facts.

I am also indebted to the Directors of Fine Art Development Ltd, Burton-on-Trent, England, Messrs Raphael Tuck and Sons Ltd, and Walt Disney Productions, for their courtesy in allowing me to reproduce material originally published by them.

My special thanks are due to Mr Tony Warr who allowed me to raid his fabulous collection of Tuck's postcards for illustrating the colored section of Tuck cards; to Mr Ron Griffiths who made available so much of his own collection of lovely American modern cards; and to Dr Charles Hollingsworth for the loan of his complete set of the *American Postcard Journal.* I am most grateful to Mr Michael Clarke, Mr and Mrs William Frost, Mrs Joan Humphreys, Mr Ken Lawson, Mr and Mrs John Powell of Ludlow, and Mr Robert Woodall for their assistance in helping me find so much of the material I wished to illustrate.

Finally I am immensely grateful to Mr Christopher Orlowsky for producing the splendid design of the up-to-date version of the 'Hands Across the Sea' postcard featured in the Preface.

[6]

PREFACE

Hands Across the Sea

A favorite theme used by picture postcard publishers during World War 1 incorporated the symbol of clasped hands spanning the oceans. These 'Hands Across the Sea' cards, as they were called, were intended to show the friendship between nations allied against a common enemy in wartime. This emblem of a warm handshake could well be used to interpret the bond that exists between the ever growing band of deltiologists divided by the seas.

Over the past few years the early twentieth-century vogue for collecting postcards has now become more of a respected hobby institution than just the revival of a bygone pastime. In Europe there are many pioneers to thank for reintroducing this pleasurable hobby, but it will

Fig. 1   A 'Hands Across the Sea' card by Christopher Orlowsky, commissioned by the author.

[7]

not diminish the gratitude due to them if it is remembered that in many regions of the United States of America there was little need for new pioneers to emerge—since the hobby there was never altogether forsaken.

By the middle of the 1940s, after World War 2 was over, American deltiologists had not only retrieved their postcard albums from their wartime hiding places, they had also begun to discover a remarkable companionship of interest in their hobby through the formation of new Postcard Clubs. The idea of having a regular meeting place where members of the American postcard world could converge to discuss and display collections, swap a few cards, maybe purchase a treasure or two, caught on to the degree where now there are not only many firmly established Clubs in the States, but also several others have branched out in far distant places from Europe and Asia to the Antipodes.

This book, then, is intended as a tribute to the deltiologists of America, a firm clasping of hands across the sea from their fellows who live just an ocean away.

Valerie Monahan 1981

THE AMERICAN-ENGLISH INFLUENCE

In the mid-nineteenth century, a self-taught mathematician and linguist from Worcester, Massachusetts, had a mission. Born in 1810, Elihu Burritt started his working life as a blacksmith, but with his extraordinary capacity for learning it was obvious that shaping shoes for horses was not to be his destiny. He was motivated by a passion for helping his fellow men towards a better understanding of each other. His firm belief was that if the ordinary men and women of all nations could communicate with each other by the establishment of a universally cheap postage system, the chances of world peace would become more secure.

A successful propaganda campaign conducted at public meetings and through the use of pictorial stationery had resulted in the formation of an industrious movement devoted to his cause in America. Thus encouraged by the fervor for his ideas for the creation of an Ocean Penny Postage scheme he travelled to England in the 1850s, where he was as sympathetically received by people in high places as he had been by his own government back home in the States.

Unfortunately, like so many other worthwhile pioneering causes, the fruition of Elihu Burritt's dream took too many years for him actually to see its maturity. He died in 1879, nineteen years before the institution of an Imperial Penny Postage on Christmas Day, 1898. Almost forty years had passed before the aspirations of a far-sighted American were finally realized by an English Member of the British Parliament, John Henniker Heaton, with the honors heavily weighted in favor of Elihu Burritt.

Just the same, this behind-the-scenes effort to simplify international communication was perfectly timed to benefit the senders and receivers of the new picture postcards—even though it took a little time

[9]

for the not so well travelled members of a universal public to get acquainted through the international exchange of postcards. However, once they caught on to the idea, there was a great interchange of postcard mail between the ordinary citizens of America and Britain. This fact has frequently been confirmed by the huge number of postcards with USA postmarks found in private British collections, and vice versa in America.

Through this novel and exciting traffic of cards between countries with no barrier of language to impede progress, the dream of Elihu Burritt came true beyond all imagining. The picture postcard had proved itself to be a triumph in the realm of early international communication; like the touch of a friendly hand in greeting, postcards with their simple messages fluttered through the private mailboxes to cement many an understanding between strangers, which were to ripen into friendships to last a lifetime.

About the time when Elihu Burritt and his associates were busy carving an important place in the archives of postal history for the institution of the Ocean Penny Post, two Philadelphians were occupied with the idea of producing what are generally believed to be the first private postcards. This was a very difficult feat at a time when the might of the Post Office was matched against anything that could be described as a private venture in the postcard line! As it happened, the first issue of the J. P. Charlton and H. C. Lipman cards never managed to get off the ground; but the second issue of Lipman cards, as they became known, with their narrow borders of colored decoration, were sold and postally used in the early part of the 1870s.

There was, however, a large quantity of government postal cards

Arthur Strauss, Inc., Publishers, New York. No. 121.

Fig. 2   A Private Mailing Card published by Arthur Strauss, Inc., pioneer publisher of New York.

[10]

Fig. 3   Early black and white vignette view of Union Square, New York, published by pioneer publisher Arthur Livingstone. From the collection of Ron Griffiths, this card is No. 59 from the 'Greetings from Picturesque America' series with the distinctive Livingstone symbol of Miss Liberty in the top left corner guarding the American Flag supported by the Eagle.

with black and white drawings distributed as advertising cards, and many of these were printed by American firms who later were to become the pioneers of the picture postcard industry when the Private Mailing Card was officially authorized by Act of Congress in 1898. American publishers like E. C. Kropp (Milwaukee), Arthur Livingstone (New York), the American Souvenir Company and Hugh C. Leighton (Portland, Maine) were among the many early producers of a fine selection of cards which have become eminently collectable today.

On the other side of the Atlantic a battle of a different kind was being waged between the Post Office and private publishing companies. In the United Kingdom, permission had been granted for the publication of postcards other than those issued by the Postal Authority. In 1894, provided the strict guidelines governing the size of postcards were not contravened, British publishers were permitted to publish picture cards; but in those early days, when the only place where messages could be written was on the picture side, there was little room for adventures in art. British publishers wanted to compete with their Continental colleagues in Germany and France, who were allowed to spread their pictures over an area of $5\frac{1}{2} \times 3\frac{1}{2}$ inches (140 mm × 89 mm) instead of having to cram them onto the court-size proportions of the British card. The argument over one vital inch in width (which was all it amounted to) raged on for four years, until Adolph Tuck of Raphael Tuck and Sons

Ltd managed to charm the British Post Office into changing its mind.

This happy state of postcard affairs in Britain coincided with the equally joyous victory of American publishers defeating the dominance of the American Post Office Authority in 1898, and the road to success for both nations stretched ahead without any further impediment to progress—apart from the small matter of how best to satisfy an ever increasing demand for the latest and most convenient novelty in communications.

By the turn of the century, demand was on the brink of reaching tidal wave proportions, and in America (as in Britain) there were too few printers who were competent to cope with large consignments of orders for postcards. So, following the example of other countries in a similar position, much of the postcard work featuring American tastes and themes was farmed out to the fine chromolithographers in Germany.

It was not long after the authorization of privately printed American cards that a number of British manufacturers began to cast a speculative eye over the vast potential offered by the American market. In a remarkably short time branches of British firms were established in the United States. Trade marks already familiar to the British public were soon to appear on cards which were exclusively produced to tempt the cents from the pockets and purses of the American public; and with pride the words 'New York' were added with a flourish to the home base of 'London' on the address side of the cards.

Neither did this early Anglo-American postcard connection end with publishing interests. Artist-signed cards were beginning to invite

Fig. 4   A black and white reproduction of a delicately colored card published by E. C. Kropp, Milwaukee. No. 2545, depicting the Santa Ana Bridge, Salt Lake Route.

Fig. 5 Early card designed after the fashion of the German Gruss aus theme. An interesting plus for this Greetings from Utica card with its triple vignette views is the signature on the front. J. C. Schreiber, Utica, New York, was also the publisher. Postmarked New York, January 1 1899, his personal New Year's greeting reached his friend in Australia on St Valentine's Day.

notice, particularly by those who were already starting to call themselves 'collectors', and the talent of American artists did not escape the attention of British and other European publishers either—whether they boasted an American base for their companies or not. Popular names like Frances Brundage, Clare Victor Dwiggins (Dwig), Ellen Clapsaddle, Richard Outcault and Grace Wiederseim (Drayton) were destined to become universally in demand in their day, and cards bearing their signatures were eagerly sought by a later generation of collectors in the course of time.

From the early 1900s there were many new names to be added to what now has become a formidable list of American publishers and artists, many of whom are well known by deltiologists the world over. A well-researched compilation of internationally-known postcard publishers and artists was produced by Barbara Andrews of Michigan in 1975. Entitled *A Directory of Post Cards, Artists, Publishers and Trademarks*, this book, published by Little Red Caboose of Irving, Texas, is a *must* for every deltiologist's bookshelf. So, in the formative years of the postcard age with new blood constantly flowing through the veins of the industry and a wonderfully thriving Anglo-American import and export trade to add a touch of international piquancy, the demand for the new picture postcards was fully satisfied.

Although it is the expressed view of many deltiologists that the fad

[13]

for collecting postcards in America had begun to pall by 1912, and was virtually dead before the first year of World War 1 was out, there are many cards to be found with American postmarks to testify that, although actually collecting them may have lost its charisma for a while, they were still very much alive as a conveniently brief form of communication.

After that first catastrophic Great War of 1914–18, postcard publishing continued to prosper in the States, producing enough cards of the type to encourage a renewed fervor for filling postcard albums—even though the interest was not to reach the card-crazy heights of bygone days. For a renewal of that dizzy stage in collecting history to arrive it took a second World War, a reckless abandonment of the hobby altogether by the British and most other European nations, and a slow emergence of a different sort of absorption in collecting which embraced a curious number of objects to stir nostalgic impulses. Among the items to be rediscovered were the postcard albums and collections of yesterday; cartons, boxes, tins, and books filled with the long-forgotten evidence of somebody else's cherished past. It took some time for the British to blow the dust off such new-found treasure before it was realized that their American friends were well ahead of them in forming the foundation for a modern-style postcard-collecting hobby, renamed deltiology. In fact, it was something of a shock to find that the deltiologists of the United States had never wholly forsaken the hobby started by their great-grandparents, but since the end of World War 2 had been beavering away stabilizing its foundation by the institution of Postcard Clubs, holding regular postcard bourses, publishing magazines and checklists, and willingly sharing their bubbling enthusiasm with anyone who showed a sparrow's breath of interest in their collections.

Now, well over eighty years on, collecting picture postcards has joined the respected ranks of the more traditional fields of collecting, and through the efforts of American and British devotees of the hobby the fascination for deltiology has spread to reach once again every corner of the globe. Once more, postcards, though modern in texture and design, drop through the mailboxes of the world with simple requests to 'My dear Friend' to exchange a multi-variety of cards with their friends across the sea. How Elihu Burritt would have loved to have seen at least this part of his dream come true!

POSTCARD VIEWS

The process of universally uniting deltiological interests has had its moments of excitement and shifts in fashion over the years. Capricious movements of what category is 'in' today and what artist or publisher may be considered 'out' tomorrow has added a dash of spice to postcard-collecting habits. Predictably, the pattern to have cast a fickle shadow over most card categories at some time or another involves themes of fancy rather than subjects of factual substance.

Depictions of early transportation of all kinds, anything to do with pioneer flight, real photocards of Presidents and Royalty (preferably caught in informal mood), and the less august cards showing ordinary people going about their daily work using their hands and archaic implements that have since been transferred to local museums, are, and always will be, on the list of desirable cards to collect. To these can now be tagged the nostalgic glimpses of the streets and places of a bygone era which are only vaguely familiar to today's generation of deltiologists.

Since the postcard industry began, views in monochrome and color have been its backbone. So numerous was the number produced wherever in the world postcards were printed and published, it took a little time for modern collectors to recognize the significance of building up collections of view cards. Now the days are long gone when it was possible to pick up bundles and boxes of cards that were considered to be too common to be collectable for just a few cents.

The hunt is on for any view that shows the slightest stir of animation or historical worth. Early main streets with their old-fashioned stores, crowds of people, and a procession of horse-drawn transportation clippety-clopping down the middle; streets showing trolley-cars, preferably in close-up; views of fire-engines and the first automobiles, railroad stations, old theaters and movie houses, and the ascent of the

Fig. 6 Embossed view of Newspaper Row, San Francisco. No. 24 published by Goeggel & Weidner, San Francisco.

Fig. 7 Anonymously published Private Mailing Card 1898. Vignette views of Denver and the Colorado State Capitol —original in color.

Fig. 8 One of the scarce 1897 cards published by C. F. Th. Kreh. These cards were in use before the authorization of the Private Mailing Card and bear the imprinted government postage stamp.

Fig. 9 This lovely card from Ron Griffiths collection showing Main Street, Bisbee, Arizona, was published by C. W. Barker, Arizona, No. 3594.

new skyscrapers—all quickly vanish into the albums of the eager devotees of topography. To these favorite scenes of long ago can be added the photocards of the well-kept residences of the famous, post headquarters, banks, auditoriums, libraries, homes for soldiers, schools, universities, city halls and government buildings, mission houses, custom houses, hospitals, and churches of all creeds and denominations. Apart from the churches and universities, so many of these buildings have either vanished altogether or have been modernized out of all recognition to the way they once were that social historians are provided with an almost endless source of variety and interest from the cards that depict them. Postcard publishers of the day made sure that the heritage of architecture was displayed from every angle both inside and out!

Enthusiasm for gathering in early postcard views is by no means restricted to a detached preoccupation of collecting only the scenes that are nationally familiar to individual collectors. Postcard views have opened the doors of the world to the untravelled many who live far away from distant places they long to see, especially children who learn more quickly from visual aids than from text books that rarely capture the romance of faraway places. Certainly, amid the huge variety of the world's viewcards there are many 'off the beaten track' sights exclusive only to the postcard medium, and therefore of greater charm to the viewer than the repetition of the stereotyped choice of illustrations so often found in travel books and brochures.

The exchange of viewcards between American and British correspondents in the early part of this century provided an invaluable service in helping to familiarize the two nations to the citizens of both. No less important are the messages written by thoughtful senders. In one album found in Britain there were hundreds of a 1914 series of cards published by the Acmegraph Co. (Chicago); all of them were nicely colored views of busy Chicago street scenes, important buildings, hotels, and scenes of people enjoying the pleasures of Jackson Park. On the reverse of each of them the sender, a Mrs Clara Williams, had carefully noted relevant morsels of information to match the pictures on the fronts. On the back of a card showing the beach at Jackson Park, crowded with private horse-drawn transportation and promenaders, is written, 'This is where our old World's Fair was held in 1893', a description which has since promoted this card to a place among the beautiful souvenir postal cards distributed by Charles W. Goldsmith at the World's Columbian Exposition, Chicago, 1893. A similar promotion into the aviation section was earned by a depiction of the Blackstone Hotel, Chicago, numbered 609 in the Acmegraph Co. series. The observation on this card was to inform that 'this is the only hotel here having an airship station'.

Fig. 10 *Underground in the Tamarack Mine, Calumet, Michigan. Published by Hugh C. Leighton, Portland, Maine.*

Fig. 11 *The writing cluttering up the picture tends to distract, but this card is a lovely example of fun published by Hugh C. Leighton, Portland.*

Fig. 12 *Sunday afternoon at the Music Stand, Golden Gate Park, San Francisco, postmarked 1908—unstamped but with a Ferry Station cachet. Published by I. Scheff & Bros, San Francisco.*

Fig. 13 *A 1909 view from the collection of Ron Griffiths showing the 'Busiest Street in the World'. Published by Hugh C. Leighton, Portland, Maine.*

On many viewcards it was not necessary for senders to add their own notes. Several publishers such as the Max Rigot Selling Co. Chicago, the Western Publishing & Novelty Co., Los Angeles, and the Detroit Publishing Company on the reverse side of their 'Phostint' series, were sufficiently considerate to acquaint strangers of the beauty and interest of different places by printing an enlightening paragraph or two themselves. A browse through a collection of Detroit's 'Phostints' is an exceptionally absorbing experience when it comes to reading the notations on the backs of those produced for Fred Harvey, a wealthy owner of a chain of hotels and restaurants. Fred Harvey made a contractual arrangement with the Detroit Publishing Company to produce a long series of cards depicting views of places well away from the beaten tracks that led to the great American cities. Many of these portrayed ethnic scenes of Indian reservations, customs and occupations. Imprinted on the reverse of each card is the trademark of Fred Harvey's name within a circle formed by the 'H'—which at first glance makes it look as though the aspirate is missing! Card No. 13989 showing a Pueblo Indian drilling turquoise in New Mexico is illustrated in Plate 72. The picture itself is interesting enough, but like all the Harvey cards there is the additional bonus in its favor of an edifying description to be read on the reverse:

'All the turquoise worn by the Southwestern tribes in their wampum necklaces, ear-rings, etc., is drilled with a hand drill. It is believed that the more primitive method of drilling was with a single flint pointed stick, revolved between the hands, but the drill illustrated, although very primitive, has been used for centuries. Turquoise is the only stone valued by the Indians and practically all of the turquoise obtained by the various tribes has been sold or traded to them by the Santo Domingo Indians, near whose village the mines are. There is no better turquoise in the world than that found in this vicinity.'

What more can a stranger to a country ask from a postcard?

Before the introduction of their 'Phostint' processing, the Detroit Publishing Company produced countless early views of exceptional clarity in colors which glowed sharp and jewel-like in definition; cards to show the quiet, well-bred dignity of the streets and buildings of Boston, others to tell of the peace to be imagined behind the ivy-clad walls of places such as Massachusetts Hall, the oldest part of Harvard University, and many more to describe places as far afield as the Mobile water front in Alabama. These early gems, whether they are published under the name of the Detroit Publishing Company or the Detroit Photographic Company, are superb collectors' items to grace any album, wherever in the world it is filled.

Although it would be untrue to claim that American and British albums are bulging with views that differ from the home-grown interests of their owners, it can be said that many deltiologists nowadays have formed the habit of including desirable cards from either country from which they would be disinclined to part. The virtue of such cards is a matter of personal taste, but in collections of virtuoso importance the quality and beauty of early productions stands out with breathtaking significance.

In America, as in Britain, the cards published by Raphael Tuck and Sons Ltd appear to tower supreme above the rest; but Tuck's were always international in their outlook, being as much American as they were British or French, basing themselves as they did in the capitals of commerce in New York, London and Paris. All the same, the British have found much to admire and engross them in the work of many American publishers, from the vastness of Detroit issues to the exclusively small number of gems published by such firms as C. F. Th. Kreh.

Most publishers developed a style which was unique to them and most are sufficiently singular for modern deltiologists to tell at a glance the origin of cards without checking the colophons or the names and addresses printed on the reverse. At one time this deltiological expertise was viewed as some sort of party trick until it was realized that this art of discernment comes with practise. The same ease of identification applies as much to the issues of American view cards—mainly because American publishers generally confined themselves to the scenes and doings of their own particular States. For example, Illinois cards are represented by the Acmegraph Co., Max Rigot Selling Co., the Franklin Postcard Company, the American Souvenir Co., and P. F. Volland & Co. of Chicago; California is headed by Edward H. Mitchell of San Francisco, the Western Publishing and Novelty Co., Los Angeles, the Pacific Novelty Co., Britton & Rey, San Francisco, and Stanley A. Piltz, San Francisco; Massachusetts is beautifully portrayed by the Detroit Publishing Co., efficiently by H. S. Hutchinson & Co., New Bedford, George S. Graves, Springfield, and E. W. Cobb of Brockton; New York by the Rotograph Co., Paul C. Koeber, Joseph Koehler, the Photo & Art Postal Co., Arthur Livingstone, Arthur Strauss (both of the latter publishers were among the pioneers of picture postcard production), the United Art Publishing Co., and the Pictorial Card Co., New York City; Maryland had I & M Ottenheimer, Baltimore; Ohio, C. G. Richey of Columbus; Arizona, John G. Verkamp, and C. W. Barker, Bisbee; Oregon, pioneer publisher E. C. Kropp, Milwaukee, and the American Souvenir Co.; Maine, another pioneer Hugh C. Leighton of Portland and O. Crosby Bean, Bangor; Pennsylvania, the Philadelphia Post Card Co., and E. A. Grimm of Hamburg; Hawaii had the Hawaii & South Sea Curio Co., Honolulu. Add to these the multitudinous efforts from

Fig. 14 From postcard series No. 2125 'Waco, Tex' published by Raphael Tuck and Sons Ltd showing an early view of Austin Avenue.

Fig. 15 View of Polk Street Depot, Chicago—published by B. Sebastian, Chicago and issued as card No. 75.

Fig. 16 Grain ships from all parts of the world in the Harbor of Portland, Oregon. Publisher's colophon difficult to identify.

Fig. 17 Early view card published by Arthur Strauss, Inc., New York, as card No. 101.

Fig. 18 1920s view of the Madison Beach Hotel, Connecticut, with some attractive automobiles out front. Published by the Hunter Photo Co.

Fig. 19 Orange-day Parade, Toronto, showing a small part of the crowd in Yonge Street, July 12 1907. Published by Valentine & Sons Ltd, Montreal and Toronto—and, of course, Dundee!

Fig. 20 Canadian Souvenir Postcard published by Warwick Bros & Rutter Ltd. Toronto. Semi-patriotic theme flanking the arrival of the Boston steamer at St John, New Brunswick.

Fig. 21 Photocard of Carters' Sleigh, Quebec, June, 1911. Published by Valentine and Sons Ltd.

publishers like A. C. Bosselman, the Curt Teich Co., the Ullman Manufacturing Co., the New England News Company, Boston, Raphael Tuck and Sons Ltd, Valentine and Sons, Dundee, New York, Boston and Montreal, and a fair idea of the potency of the American scene portrayed on view cards can be seen—especially when it is remembered that to the names mentioned there can be added a hundred or so others.

The thriving industry of producing viewcards to cover every imaginable geographical area was by no means the sole preserve of regular postcard publishers. While their concentration had to be centered upon studied arrangements of ever popular sights of buildings and city streets which were guaranteed to be sure sellers, the scope was unlimited for amateur and free-lance professional photographers to capture the off-beat scene or whatever else took their fancy. Real photocards to come from such free-lance efforts that depict disaster scenes, animated close-ups of transportation, or off the beaten track accounts of life as it used to be at the turn of the century, often command high prices today— always provided, of course, that the cards have retained a crisp, sharp quality of detail, and have not faded into a murky blur of sepia! Another factor to govern the pricing of private photocards is their comparative scarcity; unlike the product of the big card producers, the end result in experiments of good photography was restricted to the distribution of perhaps a hundred or so cards in localized areas.

A fascinating collection belonging originally to a Mr L. R. Christie OBE was recently unearthed, in which a dazzling wealth of real photocards was found. Mr Christie was an important official of a British railroad company, and among his many postcard correspondents was a Mr H. W. White who wrote on the back of a card of the Peace Arch near White Rock:

'This Arch was erected to mark the one hundred years of Peace between the United States of America and Canada. The boundary line between the two countries being over three thousand miles long, and without fort or gun—only a few cement posts to mark the line. A piece of oak taken from the old ship Mayflower that carried 120 Pilgrims from Southampton on 5th August, 1620 to settle in America was built into the concrete of the Arch. The writer had the honor of raising the American Flag at the dedication—and the names of all participants are placed in the dome receptacle.'

Information of this kind is rarely found in reference books, but this message gives an example of how postcards and their original senders sometimes help to find missing pieces in the jigsaw of history.

Apart from individual photographers using their cameras to good postcard advantage, there were a number of cards published specifically

[23]

to show the work of Camera Club members. The Municipal Art League of Chicago issued an extensive series featuring the efforts of the Chicago Camera Club with full credit given to the names of the photographers on the picture side. And although the poor print technique did little justice to the camera work, such cards have earned their place somewhere in postcard history.

Another long series of photocards was published by David Pond Willis Associates, Post Photographers, Fort Dix, N.J. during World War I. These cards informed that they were 'Postage Free to Service Men' on the reverse side where there is also a sketch of a US soldier in the bottom right corner with the words: 'For Victory—Buy United States WAR BONDS and STAMPS.' For the seasoned deltiologist, Camera Club cards and those showing views of Fort Dix with patriotic pleas on their backs will not be of much interest, but to the newcomer to the world of deltiology such cards offer an inexpensive start.

A modest starting point down the road to absorption in the fascination of the postcard-collecting hobby is also to be found in a browse through the modern section of cards. Many of the present-day variety have already been promoted from their original cost of a few cents into the dollars bracket, and can be relied upon to become the investment propositions of the future—even some of the current views. Imagine the bewilderment of an age fifty or so years hence about 'The Big Apple' card with its encapsulated view of New York skyscrapers! If the skyscrapers —or even the apple trees—are still in existence then, will that generation still be saying 'I'm Crazy About' them? Imagine, too, the interest there will be in such items as the handsomely produced books of perforated postcards published by Dover Publications Inc. New York. There must be many deltiologists who have resisted the invitation to 'Fold on perforation before detaching card', preferring to keep these books of thirty-two photocards intact to stash away as collectors' items for their grandchildren.

Viewcards, whatever their age and whether they be real photo types, artist's impressions or the mass-produced kind of photographic compositions, will always have a teasing habit of awakening the memory of anyone old enough to remember a distant past. Deltiologists are well used to the exclamations of delight uttered by their seniors in age whenever a view of special poignance to them is spotted. There are many spritely eighty-plus years young people who can remember the fun their parents had in accumulating cards for the family postcard album; people who have a store of reminiscences to unfold should some of the cards illustrated in this chapter be identifiable with the life and events of the days when they were young. Someone will recall spending a relaxing Sunday afternoon listening to the sounds to come from the Music Stand,

Fig. 22 Real photocard of the Royal Mail, French Canada. Published by W.G. Macfarlane, Toronto.

Fig. 23 Another card published by Valentine & Sons Ltd showing the Observation Car, Vancouver.

Fig. 24 'Tobogganing' High Park, Toronto. The sender of this card has drawn an accommodating diagram on the reverse to show how dangerous the slide for the 'Foxy Quiller' can be! Published by Valentine & Sons Ltd.

Fig. 25 One of the exaggerated fruit cards issued by the Canadian Post Card Co., Toronto, in 1910.

Fig. 26 'Future New York' an artist's impression of 'The City of Skyscrapers' by Moses King, with a wealth of detail on the reverse.

Fig. 27 Postmarked 1907, card 2021 of the Steel Globe Tower, Coney Island, New York. Published by S. Langsdorf & Co., New York and Germany.

Fig. 28 Photocard of the Grand Trunk Railway Station, Ottawa—and, yes, it is published by Valentine & Sons Ltd.

Golden Gate Park, San Francisco; someone else will have a tale or two to tell about what it was like to work underground in the Tamarack Mine, Calumet, Michigan; others still will travel back in time on the railroads of their childhood or walk again along Main Street of Bisbee, Arizona. Somewhere there will be a Canadian who will remember how dangerous the slide for the 'Foxy Quiller' could be—and the fun that went with the old-style toboggan ride.

Revival of interest in the search for good topical cards is universal and because so many of the early viewcards can be sub-divided into several specialist subjects sought by ardent deltiologists, the postcard dealer has more to do these days than to sort his stock into a simplification of geographical order. Easy enough when it comes to extracting the obviously good stuff that may—with luck—be found in new collections bought in for stock. Eminently desirable cards like those published by Samuel Langsdorf of views surrounded by alligator or shell borders are either transferred immediately to the safety of an album, or set aside to satisfy for a short while the demands of regular collectors. Not by any means such an easy task when it comes to the more general classifications with decisions to make about where to put what! A good street scene, for example, often encompasses a multi-interest; stores with easily definable names, horse-drawn transportation travelling in one direction and a trolley car zooming in from the other, a cart peddler of fruit or fish in the foreground, a horde of people in old-fashioned dress animating the sidewalks, perhaps a super-imposed publicity blurb for a once famous business house, and always the problems that may be lying in wait on the postal side. Who is the publisher? What about the postmark—and the stamp? Is there anything of absorbing interest in the message, or in the signature of the sender?

For the ordinary deltiologist who has only his own interests to pursue in the hunt after his own favorite subjects, it is difficult for him to understand the problems of the more conscientious dealers who spend their time trying to satisfy a thousand or more different requests—and get more kicks than cents for their pains when they fail to come up with the goods! Sorting bundles of viewcards into the classifications dearest to the hearts of deltiologists with so many different tastes is no mean feat these days—more a labor of love which often burns deep into the night for many dealers in their search for cards to reduce the eager demands of their clients—and, since most viewcards are still in the moderate price range, for very little reward. On the obverse side of the coin there are, of course, the entrepreneurs—the cowboy dealers who have flipped through the pages of any literature that gives some indication of putting a price to a postcard and read very little else to give them a reasonable comprehension of the subject. It is no small wonder that those who have

[27]

Fig. 29 Approaching Tunnel No. 3, near Ogden, Utah, on the Union Pacific Railroad. Published by Frank H. Leib, Salt Lake City. Card No. 530.

Fig. 30 One of the prized real photo-cards of 'Depot and Trains', Fairbury, Illinois. Published pre-1912 by C.R. Childs, Chicago.

Fig. 31 A San Francisco, Oakland & San Jose Railway postcard published by Paul C. Koeber Co., New York.

Fig. 32 No. 5156, New Grand Central Terminal Station, New York. Published by H.H. Tammen, Denver, Colorado.

earned the right to call themselves deltiologists as true custodians of the picture postcard feel a trifle resentful about those whose knowledge goes no further than the ability to arrive at assessing the price-tag.

Fortunately, as far as viewcards are concerned, there is still sufficient variety and interest around to suit most tastes and pockets, and thanks to the imagination of early publishers who went in for designing adventurous novelty cards to keep their industry buoyant, the assortment is by no means confined to the conventional cards in black and white, sepia, and color. Different textures of leather cards were prolifically produced with a tremendous range of subjects painted, printed or tooled on their fronts, and among the Santas, Teddy-Bears, flags, poems, and Indians there were the imprinted views. Metal cards made from sheets of copper and aluminium also sported the reproduction of popular street scenes. Puzzle cards came in the form of Deek's magic variety. These cards offered a change of one view for another when slanted in a different direction. Exquisitely colored American scenes on silvered backgrounds which glow when held-to-light, and several of the cut-out type of H.T.L. were among the many novelty viewcards produced by Samuel Cupples for the Saint Louis Exposition.

So vast was the production of views in the heyday of the original postcard era, it could be suspected that if placed end to end they would have stretched from the Statue of Liberty to Southampton, England and back several times over. In the boxes and albums of a dealer's stock and in thousands of private collections, the humble postcard pictures the world from every angle and aspect as it was from around the 1890s right up to the present day, and while much excitement is engendered by the sight of rare and beautiful cards signed by celebrated artists, they do not have the same significance as a well documented collection of viewcards—if Nostalgia is the name of the game!

ADVERTISING POSTCARDS

After the British introduced pictorial envelopes to go with Sir Rowland Hill's revolutionary issue of the new penny postage stamps in May 1840, those with 'burning causes' to promote were quick to spot a fresh and effective means of spreading propaganda to whip up fervor for their causes. From propaganda, only the lightest of nudges was needed for the businessmen and traders of the day to see the advantages of converting the idea to their own purpose.

With commendable zeal both in the United States and the United Kingdom, the pictorial envelope was used to advertise a huge assortment of wares and services. This was an exercise that could be viewed as a long rehearsal to perfect the medium of postal advertising before the government postcards appeared on the scene in the 1870s.

Officially, as far as the Post Office was concerned, there was no such thing as a pictorial postcard, but this did not deter traders with close on thirty years' experience of decorating envelopes with their advertising from adapting the new postal cards to a similar use. While some of these adjustments merely amounted to a discreet drawing of a trademark accompanied by a slogan or a brief description of what was on offer, others flaunted full orchestrations of pictorial announcement. These line drawings in black and white were the vanguard to pave the way to the colorful glories of advertising postcards when the time came for pictures to be officially allowed on their fronts. That is not to say that the government postal cards had completely outgrown their usefulness when the freedoms of the Private Mailing cards were permitted in America in 1898. The two cards in Figs. 33 and 34 are dated 1902 and 1933. Both show a brevity of purpose, and one a glimpse of the good old-fashioned business courtesy that was so much taken for granted in the pre-war era of the 1930s.

[30]

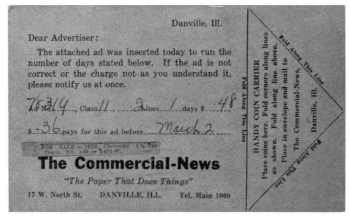

Fig. 33   *Government postal-card for the 1st National Bank of Somerset, Kentucky, dated 1902.*

The card from the First National Bank of Somerset, Kentucky, gives straightforward information to the Auditor, C.N.O.-T.P. Railway Co., Cincinnati, Ohio, with a minimum amount of fuss. The card from *The Commercial-News,* Danville, Illinois, is a classic example of how consideration for the customer was linked with a polite request for payment; but, since the 'Handy Coin Carrier' attached to this card was not folded along the indicated lines to enclose the 36 cents due, it is fair to wonder whether 'The Paper That Does Things' ever got paid!

When the objections to producing privately published mailing cards had been removed, the road to advertising anything and everything was opened to reveal a rosy prospect of a future unhindered by regulations

Fig. 34   *Government postal-card* for The Commercial-News, *Danville, Illinois, dated 1933.*

other than those which governed the laws of decency. From big business to the smallest trader, an exhaustive use was made of the best publicity agency ever to have come their way. From imprinting their names and whereabouts on consignments of postcards purchased direct from publishers to commissioning competent artists to draw exclusive designs to declaim the virtues of a mass of products, ad cards were distributed in splendid profusion. They fluttered through private mailboxes, were inserted in newspapers and periodicals, thrust into the hands of shoppers passing through department stores and drug stores, and given away in restaurants, hotels, and anywhere else where the traffic of custom was brisk. Human nature, with its innate cynicism for regarding 'free' offerings as objects of little value, more often than not consigned them to the nearest trash-can. This disregard for early postcard advertising has turned out to be a tragedy for present deltiologists who find it tedious and expensive to locate good advertisement cards for their collections.

Even so, there were still enough people with magpie instincts around in those days who helped many of the prime advertising treasures to survive; and from the sight of the ad cards to have endured it can be concluded how important the agency of the picture postcard was for product promotions in those pre-television days.

Many of the products to be seen on early advertising cards have now become household names known all over the world. The fifty-seven plus varieties of Heinz Foods, the sunshine of Kellogg's Cornflakes, and the benefits derived from drinking Coca-Cola are just a few of the temptations to be seen almost daily on television commercials. This regular persuasion to buy products which were sampled and approved by our ancestors tends to enhance the value of early ad cards portraying their original virtues, rather than to diminish it by the oversell of modern techniques. Just the same, while poster ad cards for Heinz, Kellogg's, Shredded Wheat, and any other universally known name of an American company (excluding Coca-Cola) may be cheap to purchase in the United States, they are at a premium when found by deltiologists in the United Kingdom, and anywhere else in Europe. In similar fashion, British and Continental poster advertising cards are costly for American deltiologists to buy when discovered at postcard bourses in the United States. However, in fairness, *any* postcard that can be fairly described as a poster-ad is an expensive proposition whatever the currency nowadays. To find an early Coca-Cola postcard outside a few private collections would be a gigantic stroke of luck!

Lucky finds are every bit as limited when it comes to collecting the 'Celebrated Poster' series issued by Raphael Tuck and Sons Ltd. Numbered from 1500 to 1510 there are usually six cards to be found in each set which, if this was a gilt-edged fact, would give an over-all total of sixty-six cards in the eleven sets of the series. Such a guarantee is not so simple when in sets 1500 and 1504 seven postcards have already been found, and complete listings of sets 1509 and 1510 have so far been elusive. Small wonder that the debate continues between those who assume but cannot prove exact figures of Celebrated Poster issues! Valuations for *individual* cards in this famous series vary from around $40 to over $100 according to the scarcity of each. There were many other cards published by Raphael Tuck and Sons Ltd to bear the imprint of American advertisers, either on the picture side or the reverse of the card. Butter-Krust bread, for example, used a couple of the attractive Tuck series, one designed by American artist 'Dwig', the other an exploration into the nature of 'Butterflies and Moths'.

Ad cards of the early period to have been artist-signed were inclined to earn a second look by an ungratefully prodigal public; and this was usually followed by finding a place for them in the postcard album. Among such cards was the humor of Cobb X. Shinn published by the Commercial Colortype Company, Chicago, for the Ford Automobile Company; Richard Felton Outcault's creation of Buster Brown with his girl-friend Mary Jane and his dog Tige declaring the wholesome properties of bread to the comfort of wearing a special manufacture of shoes; and the chubby, pink-cheeked innocence of the celebrated Campbell Kids invented by Grace Wiederseim (Drayton) to promote the soups of the Joseph Campbell Company.

The success enjoyed by the regular postcard publishing companies who issued cards in sets had not gone unnoticed by advertisers, nor had the craze for collecting cards escaped the attention of the ad card planners. Obviously attractive sets were of collectable value—and for anything of value a charge could be made! Promotional campaigns for a variety of products were propagated through the medium of the post-card set. These cards either carried a modest price tag or the request to accumulate a required number of coupons or portions of packaging which would then be exchanged for the postcards on offer.

In 1906, the Woonsocket Rubber Company published a set of ten colored cards priced at 25 cents. At the foot of Card No. 4 from this 'Footwear of Nations' series (see Plate 1) will be seen the advice that 'Our M. H. D. Hawkins will call on you about. . . . Save your orders for him'. The other nations represented in this eye-catching set are Lapland, Canada, Japan, Brazil, Germany, Spain, Turkey, South Africa, and Russia. (Whatever happened to the UK?) The following year, this New York Company produced a similar type of card to publicize rubber overshoes with the amusing substitution of the word 'paddle' instead of 'call' in the footnote advice.

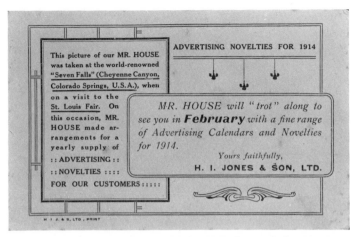

Fig. 35   Trade card issued by H. I. Jones & Son Ltd.

There was quite a rage for using postcards to announce proposed visits by travelling salesmen; although some like the one in Fig. 35 were more of the trade card type. The picture on the reverse side of this card shows Mr House astride a donkey on one of his 'trots' on behalf of H. I. Jones & Sons Ltd and their novelties in February 1914.

An exceptional series of twelve cards issued by the Bell Telephone Co. in 1910 depicted the practical uses of the telephone. New technologies concerned with electricity and sound invented by Ohio-born Thomas Edison (whose carbon transmitter helped so much in the production of the Bell Telephone) also appeared on picture postcards. Edison's creation of the phonograph in 1877 was a particular favorite for the ad card medium; although the firms bent on offering improvements to his original ideas were not always American-based. The card in Fig. 36 is an entertaining British concoction issued by Pathéphone to illustrate the efficacy of the 'Sapphire v Needle': look at the card one way and the two listeners are all smiles, turn it upside down and the reverse is the case.

For early deltiologists with a sweet tooth there were many postcard promotions for chocolate, chewing gums and assortments of sugar-coated confections to tempt them to increase their buying habits—and, no doubt, to keep the dentists happy too! Beautiful sets of ad cards for the Bensdorp Royal Dutch Cocoa firm were available from the sole importer, Stephen L. Bartlett of Boston. Not surprisingly, these cards overprinted with the Bartlett name depicted scenes of Holland and enchanting sketches of Dutch people. The Hershey Chocolate Company, like Cadbury Bros of Bourneville, England, issued many views

[34]

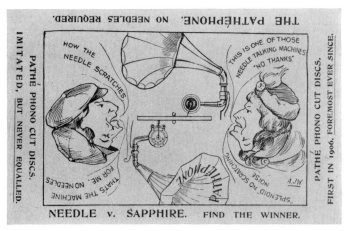

Fig. 36 Novelty card issued to advertise the Pathé-phone Sapphire for phonographs.

of the interior, exterior and surrounds of their factory. Ad cards for Lowney's chocolate were more adventurous with renderings of Indian chiefs and College girls. A delightful set of sixteen 'Cracker Jack' bears was offered in exchange for 10 cents plus one side of a 'Cracker Jack' package by the makers Rueckheim Brothers and Eckstein (Chicago) to publicize a new line of sugar-coated popcorn and peanuts.

Scenes of 'the cleanest and finest food factory in the world' were offered as souvenir cards by the Shredded Wheat people in Niagara Falls. Pretty children were used to support the nourishing qualities of Kellogg's Toasted Cornflakes, and the 'Jocular Jinks of Kornelia Kinks' promoted a taste for malted cereal flakes. The six cards issued in the 'Kornelia Kinks' set were printed in five colors and warranted to be the 'bright spots in any postal-card album'. To get hold of one of these coveted sets the 'Man and Boy' picture from the sides of two 5-cent packages had to be sent with 4 cents in stamps to the manufacturers H.O. Co., Buffalo, New York.

Newspapers and journals were hot on the postcard trail to attract bigger and better circulations. Most of their efforts like those of their British colleagues were inclined to be dreary of content and poor in quality. Cards were either inserted as a supplementary sheet in papers and magazines, or readers were invited to cut out coupons to exchange for cards as a sales promotion. Cards issued by the sheet were usually a complete set of views, and since the edges of the cards were not per-forated they had to be cut out by hand, which generally resulted in making the effort rather more homely looking than intended! The Hearst chain of newspapers did much to popularize the comic cartoon strip type cards. By 1906, the Hearst complex had issued countless cartoon cards by such celebrated cartoonists as Outcault, Opper and Schultze.

Department stores and souvenir shops published ad cards to encourage trade. The card in Fig. 37 is a postcard size trade card with a wealth of information on the front about the excitements to be found inside 'Ye Olde Curiosity Shop', Seattle, Washington; on the reverse a detailed description can be read of the joys awaiting the tourist on a visit to 'the "Evergreen" State and the "Gateway" of Alaska and Orient'.

Enticements to sample the delights offered by American breweries were to be seen on postcards for the Du Bois Brewing Company, the distributors of Hahne's and Budweiser beers; views of the Saint Louis Anheuser-Busch Brewing Associations were issued with production advertising on the reverse sides, and eight real photocards of Devil's Lake, Wisconsin, were offered free with each case of Ruhland beer. An early 1920s ad card for Schlitz ('the beer that made Milwaukee famous') is shown in Fig. 38. Published by American pioneer publisher E.C. Kropp, this card is one of the novelty variety with an enclosed flap down the center which opens out to show a colored triple view of the famous 'brown bottles' and the Schlitz Brewery flanking a full-out interior of the Schlitz Palm Garden 'Where Everybody Goes'.

Hotels and restaurants were well aware of the advantages of the ad card; and not always to show the opulence of their frontages or the comfort of their interiors. Some like the photocard in Fig. 39 of the 'Personnel Des Cuisines de L'Hotel Knickerbocker, New York' showed shrewd management policy of displaying to the world the contentment of their staff!

Steamship lines published postcards of exterior and interior views of the giant liners that sailed the oceans between America and the rest of the world. A White Star Line card (see Fig. 40) published in the USA shows the SS *Majestic*, and detailed on the reverse is all the relevant information about length, width, depth from bridge to keel and the number of 48 boilers with 240 furnaces to supply the engines. The Red Star Line produced a series of superb poster-ad cards drawn by Henri Cassiers, which are eagerly sought by today's deltiologists. Some of the most beautiful shipping postcards in the publicity field were published by Mühlmeister & Johler of Hamburg, depicting the liners of the Hamburg-Amerika line. Many of the steamship cards were issued for the benefit of passengers and a plus factor of cards posted on board ship lies in the 'Sea Post' and 'Paquebot' marks franked on the backs.

Railroad lines arranged for special issues of cards to be printed for them by the regular card manufacturers. Mainly these were views

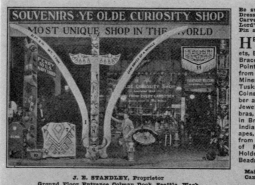

Fig. 37 A trade card bursts with information about 'Ye Olde Curiosity Shop', Seattle, Washington.

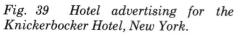

Fig. 38 Novelty card for Schlitz Beers, published by E.C. Kropp, Milwaukee.

Fig. 39 Hotel advertising for the Knickerbocker Hotel, New York.

Fig. 40 United States card showing the SS Majestic of the White Star shipping line.

The Capitol, Washington—On the Baltimore & Ohio Railroad

Fig. 41 Railroad issue for the Baltimore & Ohio company.

relating to the routes they travelled; and, depending upon the policy of the different companies, cards were either sold to passengers or given away free. For example the card in Fig. 41 was distributed with the 'compliments of the Dining Car Department, Baltimore & Ohio Railroad'. The Detroit Publishing Company secured many of the contracts for the railroads between Boston and Maine, Baltimore and Ohio, and the South Pacific and Union Pacific lines. H. H. Tammen, Denver, Colorado, was another well known publisher who contracted to print the views for the Great Northern Railway, and a miscellany of card producers looked after the interests of other railroad systems.

Mogul Engine, Latest type used by Southern Pacific Lines in Oregon.

Fig. 42 Mogul Engine used by Southern Pacific Lines in Oregon—published by Louis Scheiner, Oregon.

[38]

Fig. 43 Singer Building, New York, published 1909.

Fig. 44 Woolworth Building, New York, copyright Littig & Co., New York.

The high cost of land in the capital city centers of America forced architects as far back as 1891 to condense their plans for future building into an upward direction. The new skyscrapers with their multi-storeys carried on frameworks of steel began to emerge to welcome in the twentieth century; Fig. 43 shows a 1909 card of the Singer Building and Fig. 44 shows another of the Woolworth Building, New York. Over the years there have been many different issues of postcards to mark the importance of these two famous landmarks. A curiosity for the deltiologist who collects famous American buildings is the disparity of detail shown on the Woolworth card here when compared with the 1922 version shown in Plate 9. This latter card was purchased from the Observation Gallery at the summit of the building, and although the pictures of both are virtually the same it would appear that since 1912 when the building first soared into view five more storeys have been added to increase the footage by 42 feet and 1 inch during the ten years to have passed between the publication of these two cards.

Not all the new buildings were of skyscraper proportions, as can be seen from Figs. 45 and 46 of the Carson Pirie Scott & Co. Building,

Fig. 45 The Carson Pirie Scott Building, Chicago. Published by Max Rigot Selling Company, Chicago.

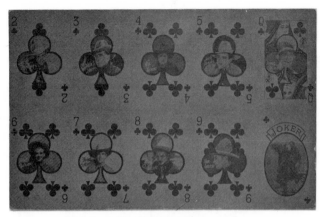

Fig. 47 Playing Card promotion post-card. Anonymously published.

Fig. 46 New Standard Oil Company Building, San Francisco. Published by Pacific Novelty Co. San Francisco.

Fig. 48 Companion card to Fig. 47; presumably one of a set of a pack of 52 postcard cards. Both these cards are very scarce.

Fig. 49 Advertising card for Mader's Famous Restaurant, Milwaukee.

Fig. 50 Ad card for 'Dodger' Beverages. Published by Dexter Press Inc., New York.

published by the Max Rigot Selling Co. (Chicago) and the New Standard Oil Company issued by the Pacific Novelty Co. (San Francisco). These buildings could almost be described as bijou by comparison to the great skyscrapers with their cathedral-like spires rising to converse with the clouds. Edward H. Mitchell, one of America's most prolific card manufacturers, also featured many of the large commercial buildings; and the Acmegraph Company (Chicago) produced a very long numbered series of hotels and office buildings, all of which have a place within the advertising section of deltiology.

Insurance companies, banks, manufacturers of everything from the homeliest of products to the very latest novelties and inventions, thirst-making ad cards for innumerable brands of beers and beverages, makes of tobacco and cigars, bicycles and automobiles, ads for gasoline, promotions of hotels, restaurants, bars, laundries, jewelers, drug stores, ice-cream parlors and everything else that could lawfully be advertised appeared with enthusiastic fervor on picture postcards.

Real photocards of contemporary actors and actresses of stage and screen were also perennial favorites with deltiologists, especially those used to promote new shows and movies. Many of the cards featuring movie stars were issued either by Hollywood companies or by the many magazines around at that time. Valentine and Sons Ltd were given

[41]

Fig. 51 The Tony Faust Restaurant, Saint Louis—the most popular place in town in 1905.

Fig. 52 A card of Lotta's Fountain, Palace Hotel, San Francisco—showing the famous murals painted by Antonio Sotomayor.

Fig. 53 A Red Letter Photocard of Charlie Chaplin on Los Angeles Beach.

Fig. 54 A view of the Westinghouse Lamp Co., Watsessing, New Jersey. Published by Charles Bradley, Watsessing, New Jersey.

*Fig. 55 The Palace Hotel Court, San Francisco.
Published by O. Newman Co., San Francisco.*

permission by Walt Disney Mickey Mouse Ltd to reproduce scenes from films such as *Snow White*.

An exciting package of curiosities was sent to Tony Warr recently (Tony, of course, is internationally known for his knowledge of cards produced by Raphael Tuck and Sons Ltd), most of which had a playing card flavor about them. Two cards from this package are illustrated in Figs. 47 and 48, and it would appear that one featuring the suit of clubs with center figures of cowboys was one of the promotional cards used to help towards acquiring the full pack of fifty-two cards plus a few jokers. On the reverse of this card is a corner intended to be clipped off as a coupon and it says: 'These coupons have no redemption value in Florida, Idaho, Indiana, Kansas, Montana, Nevada, Washington, District of Columbia, or any other State in which their use is illegal.' Then, apart from the request to 'Cut coupon on this line' and the information that the idea originated in Chicago with a US Patent Pending, there is nothing else to enlighten. Presumably the full-out example of the Ace of Diamonds with its picture of Bob Custer is one out of the full pack; but it is definitely too large to play 'Red Dog', Poker or Bridge with! If there should be a rush of information regarding these two particular cards, Tony Warr's name and address appears in the addendum at the end of Chapter 8 (see p. 115).

The value of postcard advertising still lives and thrives in the United States, and is especially useful to the smaller businesses who are not in the sponsorship league of television advertising. Some of the modern cards designed to attract new custom to restaurants and hotels are especially collectable and are usually freely distributed. The hopeful difference between these and their early predecessors is that with the present-day understanding of the value of deltiology the modern 'giveaways' will be more carefully preserved, instead of ending up in the trash-cans. It was a wise man (whoever he was) who said 'for something to be valued, it must have an original worth'! Nowadays, deltiologists are well aware of the worth of a postcard whether it be ancient or modern; thus a rich store of today's postcard pleasures, fashions, events, adventures, and advertising is being built for future generations to marvel over.

ARTIST-SIGNED POSTCARDS

Of all the two thousand and one different postcard categories to be collected, those drawn, painted and signed by their artists have suffered more dips and rises on the roller-coaster of fashion than most other card collectables. Louis Wain cats have been up-market one year and in the doldrums the next; as have Bertha Corbett's and Bernhardt Wall's 'Sunbonnets', the glowing plumage of parrots and the fruits and flowers drawn by Catherine Klein, and the enormous variety of themes illustrated by Frances Brundage.

For years the clean-cut charm of the 'American Girl' cards which emerged from the studios of artists like Harrison Fisher, Philip Boileau, Alice Luella Fidler, F. Early Christy and the rest were passed over as being too banal to be worth noticing. The same fate was suffered by Charles Dana Gibson's satirical renderings of social and commercial deceits—although the curvaceous seduction of his 'Gibson' girl cards was not so lightly disdained.

Shades of fickle fancy have not, however, obscured the fervor for the work of artists whose names have become legend in the world of the connoisseur deltiologist. The masters of art nouveau such as Alphonse Mucha, Paul Berthon, Hans Christiansen, William H. Bradley, Eva Daniell, Raphael Kirchner, and many more whose signatures on a postcard have a halo of blue-chip investment about them, will never be dislodged from the pinnacle of postcard popularity. Neither is the perception of the experts confined to the interpreters of arts nouveau and deco; they have an unerring instinct for gathering in the right cards (signed or unsigned) at the right time at the right price. At one time, this enviable intuition was used at the expense of dealers who were too plain in their anxiety to pick more knowledgeable brains to discover 'what should be put aside for future investment'. Investment was the

Fig. 56   A fine card of Charles Dana Gibson surrounded by a bevy of his fans. Published by James Henderson & Sons, London in the 'Pictorial Comedy' series.

Fig. 57   Pictorial Comedy card No. 42 by Charles Dana Gibson.

one word never to appear in the vocabulary of purist collectors; much sport was had by telling them that Louis Wain was on the wane (an appalling pun guaranteed to appal!), Kirchners had reached their ceiling, and Muchas were being reproduced so well only the experts could tell the difference! Then there was the small comfort of throwing a confidential tit-bit 'for their ears alone'; predictions, wickedly outrageous at the time, that Mabel Lucie Attwell's chubby children, Mary Golay's art nouveau flower drawings, and even the firelight romances by Alfred James Dewey might be worth their while to stash away for a future bonanza. This *soupçon* of sly fun has since boomeranged to the advantage of dealers, now that most postcards (especially those that are artist-signed) have soared in value well above the prices originally paid. Nonetheless, the deltiologist who has spent precious time researching new-found delights is still wily enough to keep his information to himself for as long as possible. No one knows better than the postcard researcher that once the name of a hitherto unknown artist is dragged from obscurity how miraculously the number of postcards bearing that signature will materialize, and how rapidly the prices for such cards rise accordingly from a minimum of cents to a maximum of dollars! However, research and the natural acumen of collectors aside, there are few dealers now who have not learned to cast a reflective eye over the signatures to appear on any postcard, whether they be known or unknown to them. With the many catalogues and books at their disposal, they have discovered the knack of valuation, whatever their new-found treasure, to within an ace of its true worth.

Apart from the capricious fancies of deltiologists for one artist or another (which were quite enough to turn the postcard market on its head and the dealers into a tizzy), there was another fashion a few years ago that was more alarming to collectors than to dealers. In the late 1970s, any card with writing on its front suddenly lost its collectability. Perfect mint cards, edges razor sharp, with not so much as an album shadow to blemish their appearance, were the order of the day. The rumor to spread like a forest fire round Europe was that this extraordinary requirement had originated in the United States where any card in less than perfect mint condition was an affront to the eyes of American deltiologists. Nor was it less strange to discover that this edict seemed only to apply to the type of artist-signed card already known to be in short supply—with or without writing on its front. It was quite astonishing how the rage for perfection caught on, and amazing how easily it was apparently satisfied. Postcards that had eluded the most dedicated of deltiologists for years past were suddenly available at outrageously high prices. Where these cards were found, and from what collections, remains a mystery. But pioneer collectors who had

[47]

Fig. 58 Pretty girl drawn by R. Ford Harper. Published by Reinthal and Newman, New York. Card No. 352.

viewed and handled a countless number of highly desirable cards in the days when 'old postcards' were trivial in value, rarely found material of such unsullied excellence among the dust and grime of the abandoned collections they rescued from the unenlightened clutches of the garbage collector!

In the world of collecting antique postcards, as in the areas of collecting the more traditional prizes of the past, age has a mellowing influence to dignify genuine antiquity. Whatever their nationality, true deltiologists may be transported into an ecstasy of delight when they find cards unmarred by the philistine use of postal equipment banged on the reverse, but since the only place for messages to be written was on the fronts of early cards with the undivided back, such 'disfigurements' tend to authenticate the early origin of a card, thus going a long way to enhance rather than to diminish its value in the eyes of expert collectors.

Fortunately, over the past year or so, the postcard-collecting scene has substantially widened for dealers to give recognition to the signposts erected by their companions in the philatelic trade, where one trail leads to the hallowed counters of the scarce and expensive and another to the cheerful availability of modern enchantments; which, given time, will be exalted to a higher plane to please future generations.

[48]

1 Card No. 4 from 'Footwear of Nations'. Copyright 1906 Woonsocket Rubber Co., New York City.

2 Californian Fruits and Flowers, published by Western Publishing & Novelty Co., Los Angeles; copyright 1912 by A. Panosian.

3 A 'Carload of Strawberries' from the Lindsey Farm, published and copyrighted 1909 by Edward H. Mitchell, San Francisco.

4 Advertising for the Prudential Insurance Co. of America — with Canadian interest.

5   One of the lovely Muhlmeister &
Johler (Hamburg) cards to publicize
the Hamburg-America shipping line.

6   British version for the Hamburg-
America line, photographed by F. G.
O. Stuart.

7   Anonymously   published   card
showing RMS Aquitania leaving
New York for the Cunard Line.

8   Superb card on silver background
of one of Bailey Gatzert's steamboats,
published by official stationer B. B.
Rich.

9   One of the cards purchased from the Observation Gallery of the Woolworth Building, New York.

11   A reproduction of a scene from Walt Disney's Snow White, *published by Valentine & Sons Ltd., Dundee.*

10   The Libby's Hawaiian Pineapple Girl, *published by Hawaii and South Seas Curio Co., Honolulu.*

12   A Poster-View of New York by A. Broun.

13 *Advertising the Olympian new Steel train, Chicago, Seattle, Tacoma.*

14 *Interior of The White Kitchen, N. Seventh Street, St. Louis.*

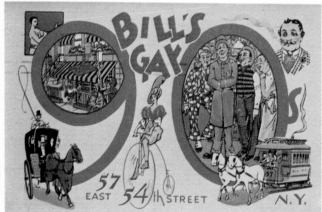

15 *Modern restaurant advertising card for Bill's Gay 90s, 57 East 54th Street, New York.*

16 *A 1937 competition postcard advertising Chicken in the Rough restaurants, published by Curteich Color and copyrighted by Beverley Osborne, Oklahoma.*

17 Card No. 177 by Grace Wiederseim published by Reinthal and Newman, New York.

19 Lightly embossed card by Ellen Clapsaddle from series No. 693, published by Stewart & Wolf, London.

18 A later Weiderseim card after the artist became Grace Drayton, published by Reinthal and Newman, New York.

20 'Thursday', one of Bernhardt Wall's 'Sunbonnet' series entitled 'Week Days', published by the Ullman Manufacturing Co., New York.

21 From Raphael Tuck and Sons Ltd 'Valentine' Post Card series No. 112, drawn by Richard F. Outcault.

22 'Leap Year' Valentine Post Card series No. 7, by Elizabeth Curtis, published by Raphael Tuck and Sons Ltd.

23 One of the delightful cards drawn by Pauli Ebner, published by August Rokl, Vienna.

24 An unusual card by Arthur Theile with a playing card theme, published by Carl Kunzli-Tobler, Zurich.

25 Anonymously published chromo-lithographic card with a ping-pong theme by Louis Wain.

26 Rare card by Rose O'Neill featuring her 'Kewpies' at Christmas, published by the Gibson Art Company, Cincinnati.

27 By courtesy of Messrs. Longmans Green & Co., one of Raphael Tuck and Sons Ltd 'Golliwog' cards, No. 1281, by Florence Upton.

28 New Year's Postcard by Frances Brundage, series No. 1973, published by Misch & Co. Ltd.

29 Copyrighted by the Edward Gross Co., New York, an 'Alphasa' card drawn by the Kinneys.

31 A card by Raphael Kirchner from series No. 123, distributed by H. M. & Co. London.

30 Copyrighted by Good Housekeeping, a gorgeous Harrison Fisher card No. 868, published by Reinthal and Newman, New York.

32 A 1905 card by A. K. Mac-Donald, published by S. Hildesheimer Ltd, London.

33 *Anonymously published card by artist Katherine Gassaway.*

35 *'American Girl' No. 40, published in the Alphasa series, drawn by Alice Luella Fidler and copyrighted by Edward Gross Co., New York.*

34 *Novelty 'Mirror' card drawn by 'Dwig' and published in Germany.*

36 *'American Girl' No. 85, published in the Alphasa series, drawn by Pearle Fidler Le Munyan and copyrighted by Edward Gross Co., New York.*

37 Early undivided back 'Heraldic' postcard No. 5015 for Boston. From the collection of Tony Warr.

38 Early Private Mailing Card, 'Chicago Series' No. 6000. (Tony Warr.)

39 Early Private Mailing Card, 'Heraldic' series No. 3006 for Washington. (Tony Warr.)

40 Early Private Mailing Card, 'View' postcard No. 5052 by Florence Robinson. (Tony Warr.)

41 Early postcard No. 672, 'Mother's Darling', by
Frances Brundage — very scarce. (Tony Warr.)

42 Another scarce card by Frances Brundage No.
645 'Babydom'. (Tony Warr.)

44 Early Valentine series No.
834 by Frances Brundage.
(Tony Warr.)

43 And yet another scarce Frances Brundage No.
661 'Little Sunbeam'. (Tony Warr.)

45 *Oilette No. 9094 'Coon Studies' by Graham Hyde. (Tony Warr.)*

46 *Christmas series No. 8457 'Happy Little Coons' by H. Dix Sandford. (Tony Warr.)*

47 *American Humor from 'Puck' Oilette No. 9412 'Coontown Kids'. (Tony Warr.)*

48 *Oilette 'Connoisseur' series No. 2816 'Coloured Folks' by Frances Brundage. (Tony Warr.)*

49 *Attractive Christmas series No. C 1035 by Frances Brundage. (Tony Warr.)*

51 *A rare Oilette 'Write Away' No. 2339 'Baseball' signed 'K'. (Tony Warr.)*

50 *Oilette No. 3553 'Louis Wain Mascots' series 3 by Louis Wain. (Tony Warr.)*

52 *From the 'Art' series No. 6298 attributed to Frances Brundage. (Tony Warr.)*

53 *Lightly embossed card from series No. 156,*
'Washington's Birthday'. (Tony Warr.)

55 *An unnumbered card to*
commemorate 'Decoration
Day'. (Tony Warr.)

54 *From the 'Decoration Day' series No. 158.*
(Tony Warr.)

56 *One of the elusive 'Ten*
Commandments' series No.
163P. 'P' stands for Protestant.
(Tony Warr.)

57 Postcard series No. 1 'Knocks — Witty and Wise' by Dwig. (Tony Warr.)

59 From series No. 6 of the 'Dry Humor' range by Dwig — 'Schooldays'. (Tony Warr.)

58 From the 'Dry Humor' series No. 5 'Smiles' by Dwig. (Tony Warr.)

60 An unusual Oilette 'A Winter Campaign', Oilette No. 9675. (Tony Warr.)

61 One of the many Valentine cards drawn by R. F. Outcault, this one from the 'Remembrance' series No. 4524. (Tony Warr.)

63 A Katherine Gassaway 'stork' card, Oilette No. 9434 'The New Baby'. (Tony Warr.)

62 One of Tuck's 'Thanksgiving' postcards No. 808. (Tony Warr.)

64 Attributed to Katherine Gassaway from the Christmas series No. 1013. (Tony Warr.)

65 From series 2, Oilette No. 9532 from the Wide-Wide World types of card. 'The Wild West, U.S.A.' by Harry Payne. (Tony Warr.)

67 From Oilette series No. 9777 'Man's Best Friend' by C. Reichert. (Tony Warr.)

66 Another from the same series as Plate 65, also from the collection of Tony Warr.

68 One of the silver-edged cards from 'Connoisseur' series No. 2825 'Silver Bridled Horses'. (Tony Warr.)

69 *North American series No. 5431, published by S. Hildesheimer & Co., Ltd, London, 'A Havasupai Woman'.*

71 *Sioux Indian Chief Red Cloud, copyrighted and published by F. A. Rinehart, Omaha, Nebraska.*

70 *A Cavendish Morton photo from Oilette series No. 1360 'Hiawatha', published by Raphael Tuck and Sons Ltd.*

72 *Fred Harvey 'Phostint' card published by Detroit Publishing Co., featuring the Pueblo Indian drilling turquoise.*

73 'Little Wooden Hut' song card published by Valentine and Sons Ltd and postmarked 1907.

75 From the same series as Plate 74. Both cards have a happy sketch of a 'going my way, thumbs up' symbol on the reverse.

74 An extremely desirable card from the 'Little Coons' series, published by Franz Huld, New York.

76 A Christmas card published by Misch & Stock, London.

77 *Official card for the Pan-American Exposition, Buffalo, New York, 1901, published by the Niagara Envelope Manufactory and printed by Gies & Co., Litho, Buffalo, New York.*

78 *Official Mailing Card published by B. B. Rich for the Lewis & Clark Centennial 1905, Portland, Oregon.*

80 *One of the colorful poster-type Hudson-Fulton Celebration cards issued by Valentine and Sons Ltd, New York.*

79 *Official Souvenir postcard for the Quebec Tercentenary Celebrations, 1608–1908.*

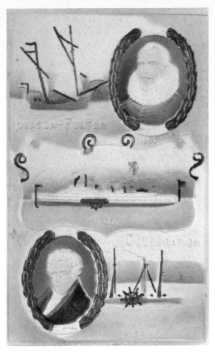

Cascade and Congress Hall.

81 (above left) Delicately colored and heavily embossed Hudson-Fulton card published by Samuel Langsdorf.

82 (above right) Colored official card published by Gale & Polden, London, for the Anglo-American Exposition, Shepherds Bush, London 1914.

83 (centre right) Folder published by the American Colortype Co., New York, which opens out to form a diamond shape of views and central advertising (scarce).

84 (bottom right) Souvenir of 'Zog' House Anglo-American Exposition, London 1914. '"ZOG" cleans Paint' advertising card.

Souvenir of "ZOG" House Anglo-American Exhibitn London 1914.

85 Benjamin Franklin card published by the Rose Co., Philadelphia, No. 954 in their Educational series.

86 Lovely real photocard of President Roosevelt and family in informal mood.

87 One of the Teddy Bear cards sparked off by the humanity of Teddy Roosevelt, President of America. Published by C. W. Faulkner & Co., Ltd, London.

88 'They all Love Teddy' Easter card published by Wildt & Kray, London, Series No. 1841.

89 *Raphael Tuck and Sons Ltd. Oilette No. 9432 'Cat Studies' by G. L. Barnes, 'Where are you going to my Pretty Maid?'*

91 *Playing card theme showing the bridge-players of Brooklyn.*

90 *Going out for a 'Katzenjammer' showing a 'devil-may-care' cat dressed to kill for a 'whatever-comes' sort of evening!*

92 *Not quite a Royal Straight Flush — but very handy for all that! My Safety Raiser, published 1906 by J. Tully, Chicago.*

93 'I'se Wishing YOU a
Happy New Year', published
by Valentine and Sons Ltd, for
Richardson & Co., London.

95 A gorgeous example of an
embossed Valentine postcard
with a playing card theme,
from the collection of Tony
Warr.

94 One of the Abraham
Lincoln Birthday cards
published by Western News
Company in their 'Flag and
Eagle' series of President
postcards.

96 Cherry decorated and
embossed Washington card
with a John Winsch back.

97 *Shamrock decorated 'Hands Across the Sea' type of St Patrick's Day card.*

98 *Your Fortune card for April, copyrighted 1910 by J. Marks, New York.*

99 *'Here I am' — Teddy Bears for Easter — published by Wildt & Kray, London, from series 1821.*

100 *'Hallowe'en Precautions', anonymously published.*

101 *International Art Co. New York patriotic card drawn by Ellen Clapsaddle, 1905.*

103 *American Post Card Number 75 published by the Ullmann Manufacturing Co. New York, 'National Cupids', card dated 1906, No. 1885 for Canada.*

102 *Flag series No. 710, copyrighted 1908 by Julius Bien & Co., New York.*

104 *Embossed 'Memorial Day' card published by the International Art Co., New York.*

105 John Winsch card copyrighted 1912, colonial type of 'A Peaceful Thanksgiving'.

106 A Philip Sanders embossed Thanksgiving card with patriotic embellishments to a fan-tailed American turkey.

108 One of the Julia Woodworth 'Cupid' cards for a Merry Christmas published by F. A. Owen Co., Danville, New York.

107 German decorated and embossed Thanksgiving card showing the turkey in the right place — on the table!

111 'Gloria in excelsis Deo' card.

109 Embossed New Year's card with beribboned lift-up flap concealing messages; published 1910 by John Winsch, New York.

110 'Santa Claus Scroll' postcard No. 525 published by Raphael Tuck and Sons Ltd.

112 Anonymously published Santa card by Louis Wain.

113 An example of one of the Mailick 'Virtue' cards for Faith.

115 Raphael Tuck and Sons Ltd rendering of the Eighth Commandment from series No. 163P.

114 'The guardian Angel' protecting her charge from danger — from the Knight series, Berlin.

116 One of The Lord's Prayer cards from Philco series No. 2254E.

117 Embossed card from Paul Finkenrath, Berlin, 'The Lord's Prayer' series No. 8415.

119 German version of the famous 'Ecce Homo' painting which has also been reproduced many times by the woven silk card manufacturers.

118 Brilliantly colored and gilded German card of the Holy Family.

120 The beautiful limited edition of the 'Ave Maria' card sold to aid the Calabrian Fund.

122 *A card published for the Wolverine Post Card Club, established in 1954.*

Angel's Flight
Post Card Club
Los Angeles, California

121 *A gorgeous postcard published for the Angel's Flight Post Card Club, Los Angeles, California.*

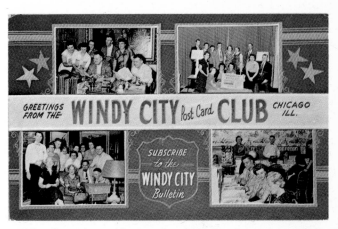

123 *Greetings from the Windy City Postcard Club, Chicago, Illinois.*

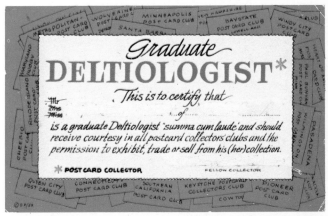

124 *One of the 'Graduate Deltiologist' cards with a montage of the names of American Post Card Clubs past and present.*

125 Peace between Egypt and Israel — *to end a war that lasted for 30 years. The treaty was signed on March 26 1979 by Mr Begin and President Sadat in Washington, with President Carter of the USA, the prime instigator of peace between the two nations.*

127 *'The Day we celebrate' — one of the Bi-centennial cards 1776–1976 from the collection of Britain's 'King of the Modern-cards' Ron Griffiths.*

126 *Moon Shot 1969, Apollo II with astronauts Neil A. Armstrong, Michael Collins, and Edwin E. Aldrin —* memorabilia *par excellence!*

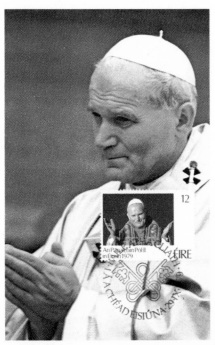

128 *The card issued to commemorate the visit by Pope John Paul II to Eire 1979, published and authorized by the Vatican.*

For most deltiological hunters after artist-signed cards, a curiosity about the lives and backgrounds of their favorites draws them like a magnet into the area of research. With this in mind, the brief biographical data of a few of the better known American artists is intended as an *hors d'oeuvre* to tempt the appetite to experiment with more adventurous fare. Examples of the work of many of the artists mentioned are shown both in monochrome and color. Even so, it cannot be overstressed that, although the artist-signed cards illustrated in this book are of an earlier *genre*, there are many modern illustrators of postcards who are well on their way to being immortalized in similar fashion in the postcard books of the future. It is, therefore, well worth while keeping a look-out for the rising talent to be seen on present-day postcards to store away for tomorrow—bearing in mind that the cards of yesterday are worth more in dollars now than the few cents of their original cost!

Philip Boileau (1864–1917)

French Canadian Philip Boileau was born in Quebec in 1864. He was the son of the marriage between Baron Charles Boileau the Consul General for France and the daughter of Thomas Hart Benton, Senator for Missouri. In 1903 Philip Boileau married Emily Gilbert, an up-and-coming actress, in New York City. Emily became his model and his inspiration for the creation of a famous series of dreamy-eyed lovelies known as 'Peggy-Heads'. Later he earned a great reputation for painting women in glamorously well bred poses. Most of his postcard work was published by Reinthal and Newman, New York.

Frances Brundage (1854–1937)

This accomplished artist started her painting career in the book world, illustrating books by Louisa May Alcott and plays by Shakespeare. From this successful beginning, Frances Brundage went on to write and sketch for her own books. Many of the well known postcard publishers commissioned her to design work for them, including Raphael Tuck and Sons Ltd. A number of her early book illustrations for Tuck's appeared on undivided back postcards and a few of the scarcer variety from the collection of Tony Warr are included in the color section.

Ellen Clapsaddle (1865–1934)

Born in South Columbia, New York, Ellen Clapsaddle designed a prolific number of postcards for numerous publishers both in the States and overseas. Her themes were mainly involved with children, for whom she had a special fondness. It is puzzling to understand why her name has not, until recently, stood out more prominently in the affections of deltiologists, for her work is both versatile and desirable.

Clare Victor Dwiggins ('Dwig') (1874–1958)

Ohio-born 'Dwig' began his career as a cartoonist for the Saint Louis Post-Dispatch. His humor on postcards is refreshingly dry and uplifting. Publishers Charles Rose, Samuel Gabriel and R. Kaplan produced many of his early creations, with Raphael Tuck and Sons Ltd eventually taking over as his major outlet. In most cases there are to be found twelve (and sometimes twenty-four) cards in each of the Tuck's sets. Titles include such favorite series as 'Knocks—Witty and Wise', 'Smiles', 'Schooldays', 'Zodiac', 'Pipe-Dreams', 'Love Potions', and many more with equally diverting names.

Harrison Fisher (1877–1934)

Originating from Brooklyn, Harrison Fisher grew up to become one of the most talented painters of delicate femininity. His idea of the 'American Girl' was always wholesome, well scrubbed, well bred, and cologne

Fig. 59   Card No. 423 painted by Harrison Fisher, published by Reinthal and Newman, New York.

scented: quite distinctly a product from well-to-do social backgrounds. Charles Scribner and Sons held most of the Harrison Fisher copyrights and his postcard material was largely published by Reinthal and Newman, New York.

Charles Dana Gibson (1867–1944)

The popularity of Gibson postcards is now universal. Born in Roxbury, Massachusetts, Charles Dana Gibson was to become one of the most sought-after artists of the day. A successful future was assured when he accepted (with becoming reluctance) commissions to draw for Collier's and *Life* magazines. In 1895 he married Irene, one of the fabulously beautiful Langhorne belles. His wife became his inspiration and his model for the delectable 'Gibson' girl drawings for a regular series of books entitled *Sketches and Cartoons* published by R.H. Russell of New York and London. Many of these drawings, among others, were reproduced on postcards. Charles Dana Gibson also found himself drawn into a firm Anglo-American alliance when one of his Langhorne sisters-in-law married an Englishman. Nancy Langhorne became Lady Astor and later the first woman to claim a seat as a Member of Parliament in the British House of Commons. Her sister Nora with her American husband Paul Phipps also emigrated to England where in 1910 their daughter Joyce was born. This much loved niece of Charles Dana Gibson was to grow up to become one of Britain's greatest comediennes; Joyce Grenfell, who gave so much pleasure to millions of people, died just before Christmas in 1979.

Winsor McCay (1869–1934)

Born on 26 September 1869 in Spring Lake, Michigan, Winsor McCay received special art lessons at Ypsilanti, Michigan, from which he was to graduate as one of the most important of America's cartoonists. Among all the cartoon characters he created, Little Nemo became the most famous, and was translated onto postcards by Raphael Tuck and Sons Ltd. McCay was also an accomplished maker of animated cartoon movies, not all of which were intended to amuse. His production featuring the sinking of the *Lusitania* in cartoon form was a sensitive and startlingly moving experience to watch.

Rose O'Neill (1874–1944)

The name Rose O'Neill from Pennsylvania is one of the most magical in the circles of American deltiology. Famed for her drawings of 'Kewpie' cards, her work is difficult to find. Perhaps a good reason for its scarcity is that, by the time she started designing cards for the Gibson Art Company in 1915, much of the American passion for actually collecting picture postcards had been temporarily replaced by a renewed interest in the folded greetings card with its envelope to hide private messages from prying eyes! Rose O'Neill also designed a series of 'Kewpies' for the Campbell Art Company's 'Klever Kard' series. These cards were clever novelty postcards with bridges punctured around the top half of the design which when broken allowed the card to be as free-standing as a folded one. Raphael Tuck and Sons Ltd also published cards in their Oilette range entitled 'Nudekin's' with little figures bearing a resemblance to the O'Neill 'Kewpies'.

Frederick Burr Opper (1857–1937)

Ohio-born on January 2 1857, Opper was one of the leading pioneers of the American strip-cartoon. He worked as an illustrator for the *New York Journal* and *Puck*, one of the favorite humor journals of the day. The cartoon strips Opper is most remembered for are 'Alphonse and Gaston', 'And Her Name was Maud', and most of all the 'Happy Hooligans' series. There were many postcard manufacturers interested in

Fig. 60 From the Water Color series No. 42 by F. Earl Christy, published by Reinthal and Newman, New York.

[52]

reproducing Opper's work, including Kaufman and Strauss and Raphael Tuck and Sons Ltd.

Richard Felton Outcault (1863–1928)

During the early part of the postcard era, Ohio appeared to be a natural nursery for budding American artists who were to blossom into fame, for Outcault was another of Ohio's sons. His drawings of Buster Brown, Mary Jane and the little dog Tige were sure-fire favorites to be seen in books, newspapers, on postcards and as promotions for publicizing numerous products. Raphael Tuck and Sons Ltd published many of the Buster Brown themes in their early Valentine card series, and Ullman Manufacturing Company issued an unusual Outcault set called the 'Koontown Kids'.

Charles M. Russell (1865–1926)

This artist from Saint Louis, Missouri, was a true master of portraying authentic Western scenes. Postcards produced from 1903 to around 1907 by Charles Russell and published by Charles E. Morris, Chinook, Montana, are none too easy to find.

Fig. 61 The Canadian Winter Girl by Alfred Bell, published by Valentine & Sons Ltd, Montreal and Toronto.

[53]

Fig. 62 'Love is Blind' by Bessie Pease Gutmann, copyright 1907 by Gutmann and Gutmann, New York.

Fig. 63 An excellent reproduction of a Charles Russell card, published 1952 by the Trail's End Publishing Co. Inc., Pasadena, California.

[54]

Jessie Wilcox Smith (1863–1935)

This sunny-natured lady was born in Philadelphia on September 6 1863. Her main illustrative work was for magazines and promotional advertising. She also illustrated a large number of books including a version of *The Water Babies* and *Heidi*. A beautiful set of postcards featuring children was published by Reinthal and Newman (New York).

Florence Upton (1873–1922)

The famous creator of the 'Upton Golliwog', Florence Upton was a true Anglo-American, born in New York of English parentage. Apart from the books she wrote, there were some fifteen sets of six postcards published by Raphael Tuck and Sons Ltd of the Golliwog theme.

Bernhardt Wall (1872–1956)

Buffalo, New York, was the birthplace of Bernhardt Wall. After fighting in the Spanish-American War he joined Ullman Manufacturing Company. His job was to design a suitable variety of pictures to help sell the

Fig. 64 Early Private Mailing Card published by Raphael Tuck & Sons Ltd. View postcard No. 5051. Drawn by Florence Robinson and illustrated by courtesy of Tony Warr.

[55]

frames the company produced. Soon after this, Ullman's entered the postcard market and Bernhardt Wall created a number of 'Sunbonnet' illustrations for them, a theme which immediately captured the imagination of the postcard-buying public. He also worked for the Gibson Company, the Illustrated Postal Card Co. and for Valentine and Sons, Dundee, Scotland. Among the cards for Valentine's he produced a very fine set of poster-type cards to mark the Hudson-Fulton celebrations.

Grace Wiederseim (Drayton) (1877–1936)

Grace Gebbie, the daughter of a wealthy Philadelphian art publisher, was born in October 1877. She was nicknamed Gigi, after her initials, and grew up to be a talented artist of well-padded children with an innocent wide-eyed look. The postcards of her work usually carry either the signature G. Wiederseim or G. Drayton (the names of her two husbands) with Wiederseim being the earlier of the two. Her most celebrated series of cards were drawn to advertise Campbell's Soups with her enchanting creations of the Campbell Kids. Among other publishers of her postcard work were Reinthal and Newman, New York, and Raphael Tuck and Sons Ltd.

THE LEGEND OF THE HOUSE OF TUCK

Pick up any postcard book, take a peek through the index and almost always the entries for Raphael Tuck and Sons Ltd will occupy more space than for any other publisher. Browse through a batch of postcard journals and it can be guaranteed that somewhere there will be found several articles written about this world-famous firm. In 1976, Sally S. Carver produced the *American Postcard Guide to Tuck* published by Carves Cards, Brookline, Massachusetts. This book, with no less than 537 illustrations in black and white of postcard themes and titles of Tuck's cards, is now regarded as a valuable source of reference by deltiologists all over the world.

By the time the sending of Private Mailing Cards in America had been authorized by Act of Congress on May 19 1898, Raphael Tuck was already seventy-seven years old, and the firm he had founded, Raphael Tuck and Sons, had become a household name in the world of greetings cards, books and all kinds of paper ephemera. How it all began is as fascinating a tale to unfold as a Hans Christian Anderson story— except that there is nothing in it of the make-believe.

On August 7 1821, Raphael Tuck was born at Koschmin, a little town in East Prussia. Twenty-seven years later in 1848 he met and married Ernestine Lissner, and in due time their family was increased by four sons and three daughters. Raphael, always ambitious for his family, decided in 1859 to move to Breslau where he felt there would be better opportunities for expanding his fine art business. A few years later the Prusso-Danish and Austrian war forced the Tuck family to set their sights on fresh horizons, and in 1865 Raphael Tuck arrived in England where he was soon to be joined by his wife and family.

Like everyone else who seeks to build a new life in a strange land, it took a little time for the Tucks to get their bearings and to learn a new language; but by October 1866 a small shop was found in Union Street (now Brushfield Street) in Bishopsgate, London. Raphael and his wife formed an ideal partnership in the business of selling pictures and picture framing.

Raphael was full of creative flair and was a perfectionist; Ernestine was an astute businesswoman with a great ability for organization and administration. With such a favorable combination of talent the business swiftly grew to form the basis of the firm Raphael Tuck and Sons.

Fig. 65   Reverse side of one of the new 'Outcault' series of Valentine postcards No. 7.

Fig. 66   From series No. 0154 'American Poets'— Oliver Wendell Holmes.

[58]

Fig. 67 Christmas postcard series 8168—1904 vintage.

After three short years the business moved to more spacious premises at 177 City Road, London, where for the next decade the Tuck family thrived and prospered.

By the time their sons Herman, Adolph and Gustave were old enough to join their parents in the business, the selling and framing of pictures had become a sideline to the more exciting activity of publishing. They began to produce fine oleographs, black and white lithographs, and superbly colored chromolithographs. Herman and Adolph were sent out by their mother on daily selling jaunts. So competitive were these trips that at the end of each day there would be note-comparing sessions, and the boy who made the best sales was rewarded with the largest egg for breakfast the next morning. The vitality of this family was tremendous; and with a father who had a continuous production line of creative ideas flowing through his head, the word 'work' was more a synonym for 'fun'.

Although it is recorded that the first colored Christmas card designed by John C. Horsley R.A. was published by Henry Cole in 1843 (see Fig. 68), it was not until the late 1860s that the excitement of sending and receiving this form of seasonal greeting joined the ranks of the more traditional paraphernalia of Christmas. American publisher Louis Prang of Roxbury, Massachusetts, and Marcus Ward, a British manufacturer, were the first pioneers in this field—with Raphael Tuck following close on their heels by 1871. The Christmas card was soon joined by a production line of special cards to welcome in the New Year; and perfectionist Raphael Tuck and his sons were fast being acknowledged for the quality and design of their work. In addition to the folded

[59]

Fig. 68 Reproduction of the first Christmas card of which only 1,000 were printed for December 1843. Designed by John C. Horsley, R.A., these cards were published by Henry Cole and sold by Felix Summerley's Home Treasury Office, 12 Old Bond Street, London. Each card was hand-colored and this example shown by courtesy of the directors of Fine Arts Development Ltd, Burton-on-Trent, is dated 'London, December 23/24'.

greetings cards, the firm was now concentrating on publishing fine art prints, booklet greetings with elaborately decorated, deckle-edged covers, calendars, and sheets of vividly colored embossed scraps to enchant the scrapbook fillers of the age.

Young Adolph had inherited both his father's genius for imaginative creativity and his mother's acumen for business. His personality was dynamic, his energy untiring. This dynamism led him to devise a scheme to make exchanging Christmas cards as much a custom to be enjoyed by the masses as it already was for those better placed in society. His reasoning was that if Christmas cards were to become a real part of the Christmas scene they ought to be treated on a far grander scale. In 1880 he master-minded and launched a national competition in Britain in search of artists with a talent suited to producing designs specially for the Christmas season. Prize money of five hundred guineas was to be awarded, and a group of distinguished members of the Royal Academy invited to be the judges. Some five thousand designs and paintings were submitted on this occasion of what was to be the first of many of the celebrated Tuck competitions, many of which were on public exhibition at the Dudley Galleries, Piccadilly, London. 1880 was also the year when the veil was lifted from the design of the Raphael Tuck 'Easel and Palette' Trade Mark with the inscription 'World's Art Service'. Dated December 15 1880, Adolph Tuck sent the following letter to a firm of agents who specialized in registering trade marks:

'Dear Sir

I enclose specimen of my design which I wish to register. My firm will trade under the name Raphael Tuck & Sons from January 1st, 1881. The classes I intend to use the design for comprise pictures of all kinds, Christmas, New Year and other congratulatory cards.'

With the business now established in the capable hands of his sons, Raphael Tuck opted for an early retirement to enjoy the companionship of his beloved Ernestine. His retirement led to a partnership being entered into by the three brothers, Herman, Gustave and Adolph, and a move to larger premises in Coleman Street, London.

Following the success of the Christmas Card Design Competition and Exhibition, Adolph continued on this trail to find the best of the new artists and writers by inviting competition in a variety of contests. Many of the new writers of those days were discovered through one of the Tuck Literary Competitions. Nor was Adolph Tuck's interest confined solely to the verse and prose of new writers. He once offered Lord Tennyson, the Poet Laureate of the time, a thousand guineas to write twelve verses of eight lines each. Unfortunately this ploy did not come off. Lord Tennyson at eighty years old was not in the best of health; but his refusal was charming enough.

This is what he wrote in a letter to Adolph Tuck:

Fig. 69 Tuck's Christmas card No. 8060 chromographed in Berlin 1901.

[61]

'You cannot imagine with what regret I have forfeited this opportunity of world-wide fame, for, beyond a doubt, these verses would have found their way into many far corners of the earth where I cannot flatter myself even my name is known.'

In the 1880s and 1890s, Raphael Tuck and Sons went from strength to strength; important branches were established in New York and Paris. And Adolph Tuck made frequent visits to the United States where he had many discussions with Louis Prang about the expansion of the greetings card market in America.

One year before privately printed picture postcards were to be officially recognized by the Post Office in Britain, Raphael Tuck and Sons was granted the Royal Warrant by Queen Victoria in recognition of its successful publication of the Queen's letter to the nation on the occasion of the death of the Duke of Clarence. This was in 1893, and in each succeeding reign the House of Tuck has been similarly honored by the British Sovereign.

Two years after the bestowal of this high honor, the 'beloved Mother, Ernestine' died. In an excerpt of a document written and signed by her husband Raphael in 1898, a tribute to her wisdom and encouragement is paid:

Fig. 70 Early Tuck folded greeting novelty Christmas card—it folds out to reveal the rabbit's head and paws protruding from the top of a Christmas stocking.

[62]

'Adolph commenced to travel in the country and the foundation was thus laid for the wholesale business, Herman taking charge of the book-keeping while the beloved Mother, Ernestine, God rest her soul, by her wise council, loving encouragement and practical assistance in purchasing, contributed mainly to the successful start thus made to the publishing of Christmas cards and New Year cards, and this loyalty assisted the now rapid rise of the firm.'

During the year in which their mother died, Raphael Tuck and Sons was formed into a private limited company. Adolph became managing director with his brothers, Herman and Gustave, as sole co-directors.

The marriage between Raphael and Ernestine had been idyllically happy, so it was only to be expected that Raphael's health would begin to fail without her companionship, and soon he was confined to a bath-chair. Even so, the gallant old man gathered enough strength to lay the foundation stone on April 5 1898 of a splendid new building designed to house all the activities of the firm he and Ernestine had founded. From the roof of Raphael House, Moorfields, the whole panorama of the City of London could be seen, and on July 6 1899 Raphael Tuck performed his last official service by its opening. He died aged seventy-nine in the March of the following year.

During the last years of the nineteenth century, Adolph Tuck had

Fig. 71 One of a set of five early Christmas cards by Tuck.

[63]

rapidly expanded the volume and variety of the firm's products. (In fact, nowadays, there seems to be no limit to the discoveries made by present collectors devoted to accumulating early Tuck productions!) Tuck's went in for publishing books and children's publications which would not only entertain and divert the young, but would also be instructive; elaborately designed and gilded scripture texts and mottoes were to be seen on the walls in many homes; reproductions of paintings and engravings of the work of leading artists became popular favorites; educational works were appreciated by the Educational Authorities; relief and art novelties to amuse were marketed in abundance, and finally Raphael Tuck and Sons Ltd entered the picture postcard field.

Tuck's first pictorial postcard was published as an experiment in 1894. It featured in the top left-hand corner a vignette illustration of the Welsh Mountain, Snowdon, and with all the Adolph Tuck flair for doing something different (and being successful at it) it was arranged for the first consignment to be promoted by mountain guides on Snowdon itself. For the next few years of picture postcard history, Adolph Tuck concerned himself with the task of persuading the British Postal Authority to allow his company and other firms already engaged in the publication of postcards to increase the size of cards to a more practical dimension than the Court card size permitted at the time. In 1898, he won his battle to bring the size of the postcard in line with the industry's European competitors, and a new era for the picture postcard began.

Supported by a star-studded cast of artists, photographers and designers, Adolph made certain that it would be his firm that played the leading role in capturing public attention in the new enterprise—but even he must have been astonished at the speed with which card-buying turned into a collecting craze. In the first decade of the new century, Tuck's published and distributed several thousands of differently designed postcards; they organized a postcard collecting club to which the world-wide membership was free to all who bought and exchanged Tuck's cards; the famous series of 'Oilettes' was introduced; portfolios of Limited Edition Proof postcards were presented in gilt-edged style as a fun investment for the future—and the well-tried practise of holding competitions was reintroduced.

The first of the postcard competitions was announced in July 1900 (see Fig. 72). It took the form of a quantitive contest with a period of eighteen months to accumulate the largest collection of Tuck postcards and the chance of a share in the £1000 offered in prizes. The first prize was awarded to the deltiologist who presented a total of 20,364 cards. In February 1906 there were three competitions being run concurrently; Competition A was the Tuck's Post-Card Chain, Competition B 'Home Decorations' and Competition C 'A Tour (Real or Imaginary) illustrated

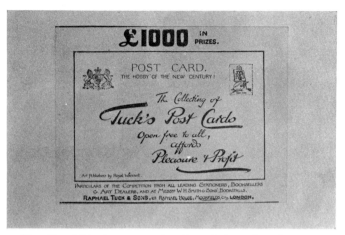

Fig. 72 This is a reproduction of the advertisement that appeared in the newspapers and magazines to announce the first quantitive Tuck competition to lure the new collectors in 1900.

by Tuck's Post-Cards'. There were 1,260 prizes totalling £6,666 offered to the winners of these competitions, £2,500 of which was set aside for the benefit of the Hospitals, Nursing Homes, Scholastic Establishments or similar Institution to receive the longest chains welded by the post-cards sent to them by competitors. All three competitions again served a period of eighteen months and became a trifle tedious in the end, so they were not as successful as the 1900 effort. A second attempt was made with the accumulative idea for a competition, just before World War 1 put a curb on such activities, and in 1923 the chain idea was revived to assist British hospitals as well as to recover some of the pre-war interest in Tuck's postcards. One of the chain cards for the 1920s contest is shown in Fig. 73; the idea was for competitors to give their favorite reason for sending postcards and at the same time give the name of the hospital of their choice. The writer of the one illustrated chose St. Dunstan's, the hospital for the blind, and wrote beneath:

'A Postcard sent and one received
 cements a friendship scarce conceived.'

This little ditty has caused much amusement for present deltiologists! In Fig. 74 is one of the Tuck's Post-Card Blotters which folds out to give all the information for the chain competition in 1906. These were inserted in all the packets of Tuck's postcards at that time.

In 1901, Raphael Tuck and Sons Ltd became a public company. The board of directors had two additions to the names of the three Tuck

Fig. 73 *The reverse side of one of the entries of postcards sent to Tuck's in 1923 for the competition to aid hospitals.*

Fig. 74 *A sheet of the printed blotting paper inserted in with the packages of Tuck's sets to advertise the trio of 1906 Postcard Competitions.*

brothers, Alfred Parsons A.R.A. was one, and Sir Arthur Conan Doyle M.D. (of Sherlock Holmes fame) the other. By this time, the sons of Adolph and his wife Jeanetta were growing up to take a keen interest in the family business. In the early 1900s Reginald the eldest was already involved in the firm, and by 1910 he was followed by his brother Desmond. This was the year for another honor to be conferred upon their father; he was created a baronet of the United Kingdom on July 19 1910.

There seemed to be no end to the imagination of the Tuck family; the name Tuck had only to be mentioned for it to be immediately identified with the highest quality of fine art printing and publishing. Limited editions of books were now included in their program; each *edition de luxe* was limited to one thousand copies and each copy was individually numbered. Contributions were made to special occasions like the Charles Dickens Centenary in 1912. For this event a unique Testimonial Stamp was published as a Centenary Book Plate for the public to affix in the volumes of Charles Dickens works in their possession. The issue of stamps (a fund-raising exercise to benefit the novelist's descendants) was engraved and printed direct from steel plates onto hand-made paper by Tuck's.

Following in the venturesome footsteps of his father Sir Adolph, Desmond Tuck arrived in the United States in 1913 to introduce to a large American concern the idea of personal Christmas cards over-printed with the names and addresses of the senders. The Americans rejected the idea. People in the States, they argued, would never send out cards unless they were personally signed. But this particular idea did not end there. When World War 1 started, Reginald Tuck went into the Army and Desmond was seconded to the French Air Force, then to the Royal Flying Corps. After the war, the two young Tucks returned to the family business. Only then did Desmond learn that his pre-war visit to the States had not been as fruitless as was at first supposed. The United States had decided to think again about his ideas for personal Christmas cards and had launched them with enthusiastic success.

All through the 1920s period it was business as usual. In the mid-1920s the charming tradition of sending St Valentine's cards was revived, at the suggestion of Lady Tuck, to celebrate the firm's Diamond Jubilee, a revival which was to be the last of Sir Adolph's enterprises. He died in July 1926. Sir Arthur Conan Doyle, who was still a director of the firm and a friend of many years, described Sir Adolph in these words: 'Behind the coat of steel there was a heart of gold.'

Until 1937 when he retired, Gustave Tuck took over as Chairman and Managing Director, then Sir Reginald Tuck and brother Desmond became joint Managing Directors in time to face together the somber period when once again the clouds of war loomed and broke in the coming of World War 2. At this time, the fortunes of the company were, like many others after the years of the Depression, at a low ebb. Yet, in the words of Sir Winston Churchill about another matter, there are those who still live to recall that in many ways this period in the history of the House of Tuck could well be remembered as its 'finest hour'.

Just after Christmas 1940, on December 29, German bombers turned the City of London into a raging inferno; and in the light of the grey dawn could be seen the empty shell of Raphael House. During that night Desmond Tuck had rushed from his home to Moorfields to see if anything could be rescued. He had dashed into the burning building but managed only to grab a few things, including the framed Royal Warrants of appointments granted to the firm through four reigns. Another precious survival from this monstrous onslaught was the air-tight glass jar laid in the foundation stone forty-two years before by the 'beloved Father' Raphael. The jar itself was damaged, but the contents were intact. They included items from a period long ago: periodicals, a catalogue of Raphael Tuck and Sons products, a greeting card or two, the results of the Tuck Literary and Painting Competition of 1894, a gold sovereign and other currency of the period, a brief history of the firm up to the time the foundation stone was laid, written on parchment by Adolph Tuck, and copies of *The Times* and the *Daily Telegraph* dated April 5 1898. Everything else was in ashes; the records of seventy-four years of dedicated industry had gone, the stores of pictures had gone and so had all the materials intended for future publications. But the spirit of Raphael Tuck and Sons Ltd had not gone—even though it meant that the firm had to start all over again from scratch. Premises were found in Appold Street in East London for some of the Tuck departments; others went to a building in the Cromwell Road, West London. Suppliers of materials rallied round, and stage by stage, despite all the restrictions, shortages, and general wartime difficulties, the House of Tuck recovered.

Since those wartime days there have been many changes in the running of the company. In the late 1940s there were a number of developments, including new marketing and production techniques and the introduction to the British public of American-designed greetings cards. Raphael Tuck and Sons Ltd is now based in the prosperous beach resort of Blackpool, England; and no longer is it the family concern of the Tuck family but a company with a much cherished name working under the umbrella of Fine Arts Development Ltd, Burton-on-Trent, England. Although the publishing of picture postcards is no longer included in the program of the modern House of Tuck, the quality and standard of what is produced remains the same—and so does the pride of those who now follow in the footsteps of old Raphael, his wife Ernestine, their sons and their grandsons.

Over a century of achievement and enterprise was covered by a family who knew its business and stretched out its arms to encompass the world, a family whom the United States adopted as one of its own. In true family tradition it was the concern of Raphael Tuck and Sons Ltd, from their treasured base in New York, to see that the customs and tastes of America were always in the forefront of whatever was planned. The legend of the House of Tuck lives on in the United States as it does in Raphael's other adopted country, the United Kingdom, through the many collectors both old and new who search the world for early treasures first created by the man from Koschmin, a little town that used to be in East Prussia all those years ago.

AMERICAN POSTCARD MEMORABILIA

In the days when browsing through cartons of old postcards was looked upon as a pursuit for the 'simple-minded', it was easy to allow oneself to be transported from one country to another or to be swept away by the dramas and events of civilizations long since past, merely at the flip of a postcard. For the present breed of deltiologists, collecting picture postcards has become a well-ordered process of methods to distinguish one card from another; and a healthy proposition for dealers who have at last recognized the glitter of gold peeking through the clutter in their junk-yards. But in the unenlightened days of the mid-1940s and early 1950s a box of old cards to the quaint few who enjoyed a good rummage was a ticket to ride on a time machine—practically free of charge and no questions asked!

The ideal was to find a junk store with an obliging proprietor who was only too glad to be rid of albums and cartons of cards for a few cents a time. With a wit more cunning than 'simple-minded', wily postcard collectors would carry off their treasure with an inward glow of antici-patory hours of secret pleasures ahead. Of course, the fun in those days was that no one knew what card would turn up next; not that it mattered, for the days when the worth of a card was to be measured in dollars were still in a hazy future. It is difficult to remember that, once upon a time, Mucha's and Kirchner's, scarce advertising and exposition cards, photocard close-ups of transportation, early aviation and railroad cards and many other such desirables were set aside as nonchalant swaps. Seasoned deltiologists often have a wry tale to tell of the wonders they found (and did not then recognize) in those musty old boxes they rescued, and the abandon with which they dispersed them among a trickle of collectors with whom they had become acquainted on their carefree travels. But then no one ever dreamed of a time when postcard trivia would be dragged into the limelight, clinically sorted into narrowly defined categories, and sold as an investment frivol to the highest bidders. The memory of those absorbing times when hours flew like seconds while fingers gradually darkened with the gathering dust of ages handled piece after piece of postal card history in sepia and color will linger forever in the minds of the pioneer collector of picture postcards, when only the sudden crick in the back of the neck jerked its owner back to the present with the reminder that tomorrow was another day for travelling into the past.

It is sad that the deltiologists of today will never know the same excitement of discovery; never know the thrill of finding a rare Exposition card nestling among a handful of common greetings, nor the revelation of cards scattered any old where in a carton which eventually unmask themselves as being parts of a complete set. The subjective ponderings over artists and publishers and printing techniques are not the same today as they once were; but that is not to say that there is little left to ponder over. Time being the enemy of most people, today's deltiologists are content to streamline their collections to suit their own taste; and consequently each collection has its own brand of unique charm and scope for research for those who can find the leisure.

Before the ever-open eye of the television camera scanned the world

Fig. 75 Balloon Route Excursion card from Playa del Rey, California.

to bring instant news into everybody's living room the picture postcard provided a matchless service of communication. The merest whisper that someone, somewhere, was planning to perform some spectacular feat would alert the postcard photographers to scurry to the front of the queue of onlookers to record whatever there was to record, and in good reporting tradition the result of their work would be on sale at the postcard kiosks early the next day. Important commemorative occasions were given the full postcard treatment; and, like moths to an arc-light, cameramen were fast on the scene when disaster struck.

Nowadays, most postcards bordering on the theme of memorabilia are neatly filed under specialized headings or in the wider slot conveniently called 'social history'. Even so, it is often as well to let the fingers travel through the cheap boxes of dealers' miscellanea to find the odd gem like the card in Fig. 75. The writing scrawled all over the front is a trifle distracting, and quite clearly the dealer from whom it was originally purchased was clueless about its classification with its angling and advertising connotations. In fact, this card is a Balloon Route Excursion card. On the reverse side there is a facsimile of a huge balloon hoisted over an open-sided trolley-car. From this a collection of pennants stream out to announce: '1$ No more. Visiting 10 Beaches—8 cities—70 miles—7 hours—6 Free Attractions—National Soldiers

INDIAN "BIG WILLIS" HOOPA, CAL.
From Photo. by A. W. ERICSON, Arcata, California

Fig. 76 Real photocard of the Private Mailing Card, 1898 era, published by Ericson Bros, California.

[72]

Home—Best in the Whole Round World.' The message written on the front informs that, as well as a seven-hour trip round ten beaches and eight cities with many other diversions thrown in, passengers were each given sixteen free souvenir postcards by the conductor to send to their friends. Not bad for a dollar! It is a pity that the balloon was only a gimmick for there are no less than four different postmarks on the reverse of this card!

Old Western movies to be seen on television make for compulsive viewing all over the world. Almost always the cowboys are the good guys and the Indians the 'baddies' to look out for skulking over the hill —rough justice when it is remembered that the Indian tribes were the aboriginals of America long before the European 'palefaces' set foot on its shores. As well as the Detroit issues of Indian life portrayed under the Fred Harvey banner, there were many publishers who recorded the ethnology of early American groups, the hard-working pride and customs of tribal Indians, and the labors and lovable humor of the black community. Raphael Tuck and Sons Ltd published an early series No. 2171 of 'Indian Chiefs' with romantic names like Chief Iron Owl and Chief Black Thunder; a set of the colorful dress of 'Indian Women' (No. 2437); an exciting glimpse of the intricacies of the 'Moqui Indian Snake Dance' in set No. 2472; a couple of brightly colored sets in their Oilette range to illustrate Longfellow's legendary poem 'Hiawatha', and many more to describe life as it was in the early days of the Wild West.

There were also many interesting photocards like the two in Figs. 76 and 77. Both of these cards are pre-1900. Indian 'Big Willis' Hoopa, of

Fig. 77 Another Private Mailing Card showing cotton-picking in Memphis, Tennessee. From the collection of Tony Warr.

Fig. 78   Transportation of cotton by road.

California, photographed by A. W. Ericson of Ericson Bros (Arcata), stands to attention, fearless of eye in obvious recognition of the importance of the occasion. The vignette picture on the Souvenir of Memphis, Tennessee, card by an anonymous publisher tells of the labors of cotton-picking. Many more such cards are featured in the color section, including a couple from a scarce set published by Franz Huld (New York), in 1900, entitled 'Little Coons'.

A small but compact collection of interesting American memorabilia is owned by British deltiologist Mrs Joan Humphreys. All these cards were sent by Father Gus Fesenmeyer, a Franciscan monk, to his parents in Peckham, London, England. The attraction lies not so much in the pictures but in the messages he wrote. On a card advertising the Willits Mercantile Co. (California), he wishes his family a Happy Easter, thanks them for copies of the *Daily Sketch*, and then goes on:

'I notice the Suffragists are still keeping up their course of violence. If Pankhurst & followers choose to starve themselves to death in prison, they should be left to do so—in my opinion!'

Not a very charitable thought, coming from the home of the Franciscan Capuchin Fathers, St Anthony's Mission, Mendocino, California.

On others he refers to the strangely severe weather in California in January 1913, with ice over half an inch thick, and on a card showing a view of the Lumber-yard and Wharf, Albion, California, he mentions how dangerous it is to drive down the steep hill there, especially if the horse is inclined to shy. But the most interesting is the card dated May 19 1906 where he says:

[74]

Fig. 79 Fifth Street in winter, Calumet,
Michigan. Published by O. Tyler.

'Severe earthquake yesterday at 5.7 a.m. in Mendocino 4 miles along
the coast. I got a good shock. Father Modestes & myself went the
rounds to view the wreckage in the town.'

This was perhaps not as dramatic or as horrifying as the many actual
photocards showing the devastation of the great San Francisco earthquake that happened exactly one month before like the one in Fig. 80,
a card published by Adolph Selige Publishing Co. (Saint Louis). There
were many similar cards published at that time by the Rieder-Cardinell
Co. (Los Angeles), the Souvenir Post Card Co. (New York), whole sets
published by Hearst newspapers, and the Rotograph Co. produced a
number of colored photocards.

Cards showing unusual scenes of fire, flood, massive snowfalls,
damage by earthquake and hurricane, automobile and train accidents,
and plane crashes are filed under the universal heading of 'Disasters'
and are readily snapped up when found by deltiologists today. Fortunately, the photographing of disturbing scenes of memorabilia was
not too frequent an occurrence for postcard publishers, who naturally
preferred to plan their schedules in advance.

When it came to the coverage of major American Expositions and
Celebrations, plenty of warning was given to the publishers who were

[75]

3238 Ruins vicinity Call Bldg. San Francisco,Cal.

Fig. 80 Card No. 3238—ruins vicinity Call Building, San Francisco earthquake disaster. Published by Adolph Selige, Saint Louis.

franchised to produce souvenir cards for an event. Cards to commemorate the World Columbian Exposition in Chicago, 1893, preceded the Private Mailing Card by five years. Official postcards were printed by the American Lithographic Company (New York) and distributed by vending machine in pairs for 5 cents a go. The agent for these cards was Charles W. Goldsmith, who also offered an alternative to the slot machine venue by selling the full set of ten cards in wrappers for 25 cents. The Columbian Exposition opened on May 1 and closed on October 31; and with so many months to play with it was not long before sets of anonymously published cards found their way into the Exposition area.

Two years later, in 1895, plans were unfolding for the Trans-Mississippi and International Exposition which was held in Omaha, Nebraska, from June 1 to October 31 1898. Official postcards were issued by the Chicago Colortype Co. By this time the picture postcard had come into its own and unofficial cards were permissible. The Albertype Company (Brooklyn) issued a set of sixteen Trans-Mississippi viewcards of the various buildings and grounds.

In the summer of 1901 from May 1 to November 2 the Pan-American Exposition was held in Buffalo. Again a set of ten official cards was authorized, published by the Niagara Envelope Manufactory and

1247 *Town Hall, Meriden, Conn. After the fire, February 14, 1904.,*

*Fig. 81   Town Hall, Meriden, Connecticut, after the
fire, February 14 1904. Published by the Illustrated
Postcard Co., New York.*

printed by Gies and Company, Buffalo, New York. There were also
many unofficial card attractions to be found at the Pan-American
Expo, including sets published by Arthur Strauss (New York) and the
Albertype Company (Brooklyn).

In 1904 it was the turn of Saint Louis to hold a World's Fair. Known
as the Louisiana Purchase Exposition, this Fair stretched over some
1,270 acres, taking in the campus of Washington University and part
of Forest Park. From April 30 to December 1 over 12,000,000 people paid
to view the hundreds of exhibits. The concession to publish official
postcards for this Exposition was given to Samuel Cupples Envelope
Company (Saint Louis), and for the first time the 'rule of ten cards' was
broken. From drawings signed by H. Wunderlich printed in glorious
color on silver backgrounds, numerous photoviews, a set of delicate
cards with an egg-shell type finish, black and white moonlight scenes,
to an array of fabulous cut-out hold-to-light cards, Samuel Cupples
Envelope Company left little room for outside publishers to manoeuvre.
Just the same, this marvellous enterprise did not stop firms like the
Rotograph Company (New York), Raphael Tuck and Sons Ltd, Dr
Trenkler (Leipzig), W. G. Macfarlane (Toronto), Adolph Selige (Saint
Louis) and many other publishers from producing many collectable
items of their own. By this time in the chronicles of postcard history, the
exhibitors themselves had caught on to the advantages of using post-
cards to promote their offers; so the deltiologists visiting the Louisiana
Purchase Exposition were well served with free postcards as well.

From June 1 to October 15 1905 the Lewis and Clark Centennial and

Fig. 82 California Alligator Farm, Los Angeles, California. Published by Curt Teich & Co. Inc., Chicago.

American Pacific Exposition and Oriental Fair was held in Portland, Oregon. This was to honor the hundredth anniversary of the exploration by Captains Meriwether Lewis and William Clark of Oregon country. As far as official postcards went it was back to the 'rule of ten'; although the flair for printing bright colors on silvered backgrounds introduced by Samuel Cupples Envelope Company had been noted sufficiently to copy. B. B. Rich (Portland) was the publisher of the Lewis and Clark Centennial cards. Publishers to issue unofficial postcards included Edward H. Mitchell (San Francisco), Lowman and Hanford (Seattle) and Adolph Selige (Saint Louis).

The Jamestown Tercentennial Exposition came next in the American Expo diary. Covering a 500-acre plot at Sewell's Point near Norfolk, Virginia, the Jamestown Exposition ran from April 26 to November 30 1907. The franchise to produce souvenir cards on this occasion was given to the Jamestown Amusement and Vending Company Inc., Norfolk, Virginia. There were some 187 cards subdivided into sections of photoviews, depictions of the American Revolution, the Spanish-Civil War, the Civil War, and, as if seeking some kind of benediction, a great variety of historical churches. Raphael Tuck and Sons Ltd, A. C. Bosselman and Company (New York) and the Illustrated Postal Card Company (New York) were among the other publishers to record the activities at the Jamestown Exposition. As was becoming the norm, there were plenty of ad cards to be given away free by the exhibitors.

Seattle, Washington, was the next place on the agenda for an important Expo event. The Alaska-Yukon-Pacific Exposition ran from June 1 to October 26 1909. Official cards, of which the principal set consisted

[78]

of around 157 colored photoviews, were published by the Portland Post Card Company, Portland, Oregon and were printed by several different firms including E. C. Kropp (Milwaukee) and Regensteiner Colortype (Chicago).

For two weeks in the fall of 1909, New York City and the State of New York put on a tremendous show to celebrate the 300th anniversary of Henry Hudson's discovery of the Hudson river, and, as a century had passed since Robert Fulton had successfully navigated the Hudson by steam, the two names were combined to form the Hudson-Fulton Celebration. A set of seventy-two colored cards were issued by Redfield Brothers Inc. (New York City) as official souvenirs; Valentine and Sons Ltd (Dundee) commissioned Bernhardt Wall to design six colorful poster-type cards; Samuel Langsdorf and Company (New York) issued a set of twelve pastel-colored and heavily embossed cards on thick board; and Joseph Koehler published another set of embossed historical scenes. The American Colortype Company (New York) published some attractive folders which opened into a diamond shape of colored views flanking a central space for use by advertisers such as the Consumer Brewing Co. of New York. These folders also printed a comprehensive program of events on the reverse side.

In August 1914, when worlds both old and new were soon to become involved in a World War catastrophe, the Anglo-American Exposition was opened at the White City in Shepherds Bush, London, England. For a few cents entrance money, the British were introduced at last to the many American treats which otherwise they would not have seen.

Fig. 83   American Army landing in France—one of the fund-raising cards for the National Federation of Discharged and Demobilized Sailors and Soldiers.

[79]

Each day there were 5,000 seats reserved free for visitors to watch the magical '101 Ranch Real Wild West' show. Among the host of other American attractions were the Coney Island Zoo, a fantastic model of the Panama Canal, The Piccaninny Band, models of the Grand Canyon Railroad and Car Station, the American Song Parlor, and the Hawaiian Entertainers. Official cards were on sale at the Gale & Polden Kiosk. Most of these were ordinary sepia views of little merit, but to alleviate the dullness there was also an attractive colored set of framed Exposition buildings, flanked either side by the national flags of America and Britain and surmounted by the American Eagle. Another interesting card of collectable virtue to be published by Gale & Polden is a black and white portrayal of the Piccaninny Band. As well as the official issues of cards for this Exposition (each bearing a circular Anglo-American Exposition postmark franked on the address side), there were some fine monochrome scenes of the 101 Ranch Wild West Show, and a number of advertising cards to be had for the asking.

The Panama-Pacific International Exposition to commemorate the opening of the Panama Canal was held in San Francisco from February 20 to December 4 1915. Cardinell-Vincent (San Francisco) was the official concessionaire for a large number of cards produced for this Expo. In both color and sepia, these cards were printed by Curt Teich.

While all these major affairs were taking place or being planned, there were many local events to interest, many of which were immortalized on postcards. Industrial Expositions were held at Cleveland, Ohio Valley, Pittsburgh and Rochester; flowers and fruit were rep-

Fig. 84 Expositions keeping their hand in with the Golden Gate International Expo, 1939, San Francisco. Published by Stanley A. Piltz, San Francisco.

[80]

resented at the Santa Clara County Rose Carnival, the National Orange show at San Bernardino, California, the Gravenstein Apple Show at Sebastopol, The Tournament of Roses in Pasadena, the Portland Rose Festival, Oregon, and the Floral Fete and Carnival, Saratoga, New York. The Albertype Company (Brooklyn), the Benham Indian Trading Company (Los Angeles), M. Reider (Los Angeles) and the Western Publishing and Novelty Company were among the several publishers who publicized these events on cards.

Fig. 85   A view of the Temple of Music with insets of President McKinley and Mrs McKinley to mark the place where he was assassinated.

Mingling with the crowds that thronged the Pan-American Exposition at Buffalo on September 14 1901, an assassin with a gun in his pocket threaded his way to the Temple of Music Building, and there he shot dead the American President. Photocards of the place where President McKinley met his death and others of his Milford home served to perpetuate his memory more than the few postcards of him ever did while he was alive. The previous year he had been re-elected as President, but little postcard notice was paid to the Presidential campaign. In those early days of picture cards, publishers had not got around to the business of photographing *ad nauseam* the President and his family, either formally or informally.

President McKinley's successor, however, came in for a great deal of attention, courting the imagination of card publishers in more ways than one. For example, it could be wondered whether small children would ever have had a Teddy Bear to cuddle if it had not been for President Theodore Roosevelt. The story goes that on a bear-shooting

Fig. 86 President Theodore Roosevelt. Published by Arthur Livingstone, New York.

Fig. 87 Modern card of President John F. Kennedy. Published by Tichnor Bros, Inc., Boston, Mass.

trip in Mississippi in the fall of 1902, Roosevelt came across a small bear cub. So appealing was this cuddly bundle of fur that he held his fire. Photographs of him with the cub at his feet appeared in the press. Berryman, one of the top American cartoonists, drew a sketch of the happening called 'Drawing the Line in Mississippi'. Public imaginations thus captured by this endearing side to their President inspired Berryman to use the bear cub for a series of cartoons. Morris Michton, a Mississippi hand-made toy and candy manufacturer, made a copy of the cub out of soft brown plush, put it on display and sold it. He called his creation 'Teddy's Bear' and when he found an increasing demand for his new type of cuddly toy he wrote to the President for permission to use his name to promote them. Permission was given and the new Teddy Bears soon became the most popular newcomers to invade American nurseries. A few years later, a German Teddy Bear was on show at a Leipzig Fair made by a dressmaker who ran a hand-made toy animal business as a side-line. So successful were the teddies made by Margaret Steiff that she soon found herself involved in big business. From then on, the Teddy Bear was immortalized in books such as A. A. Milne's *Winnie the Pooh*, and set after set of cuddly Teddy Bear designs rolled off the postcard production lines with practically every well known publisher in on the act.

Fig. 88 Le President Wilson. Copyrighted by Underwood & Underwood, New York, published in France by Levy Fils et Cie, Paris.

Fig. 89   Sir Wilfred Laurier—the first French Canadian to become Prime Minister of Canada (1896–1911).

By the time the 1908 Presidential Election campaigns came round the postcard press was fully geared to play a part in the election razzmatazz. To compete with Roosevelt's teddies, a little animal named 'Billy Possum' was invented to support William Howard Taft—and with or without the aid of the new furry invention Taft became President in 1909. Most of the fifty or so different postcard manufacturers involved in this presidential combat played safe, however, by issuing formal portraits of the contenders with suitably patriotic decoration.

Apart from the political mileage to have been gained from the postcard depictions of Presidents, the women Suffragists did not entirely escape attention. Some twenty odd years before Britain's Emily Pankhurst organized the British Suffragette movement, two American women, Susan B. Anthony and Adèle Clark, were already on the move with their Suffragist campaigns in the States. Up and down the country they co-opted the interest of women with courage enough to withstand the jeers of men. The National American Woman Suffrage Association, formed in 1890, managed to make satisfactory progress when up to the turn of the century women were given the right to vote in Colorado, Idaho, Utah, and Wyoming. Around this time, Mrs Pankhurst was marshalling her forces in Britain, but the news of the violence that was soon to emerge from the Suffragettes had no appeal for the American Suffragists. They deplored militancy; not for them was the extreme action of smashing windows, setting light to mailboxes, or chaining themselves to railings. American activity was confined to the gentle persuasion of getting the message across at open-air meetings and through the Suffragists' paper, the *Woman's Journal*, for which a license had to be obtained as 'Hawkers and Pedlars' to sell it, mainly in Boston. Even so, their British Suffragette sisters had some impact. In 1911, Emily Pankhurst visited the States to give a lecture tour, and it was not long after when the American Suffragists were organizing marches, picketing the White House to show the President that they meant business, and, despite the jeers, making life as difficult as they could for men. The cause of the suffragists was well to the front on postcards—democratically balanced between the work of male chauvinist artists like Walter Wellman with his cruel lampoons of female harridans trying to take over what everyone knew was 'a man's world', and Rose O'Neill's rare 'Kewpie' card with the plea to 'Vote for our Mothers', and similar cards drawn by women for women, thus seeing that fair play was well satisfied. Today, of course, any card to do with the early battles for the rights they won and were entitled to win are at a premium, and predictably the real photocards of newsy scenes and the heroines of the first 'Women's Libbers' are scarce to find.

That cloven-hoofed, fork-tongued, horn-headed demon called *drink* still manages to attract like the Pied Piper a merry following, despite the early efforts of Temperance societies, such as the Independent Order of Rechabites (and Rechabite cards are beautifully printed and designed), and the later censure of the American Prohibition laws. As early as 1917, legislation in America had imposed an alcoholic 'dryness' in several States; by 1920, prohibition was total, and for thirteen years until 1933 the experiment soldiered on in the face of inevitable defeat. It was a brave attempt by the Temperance Movements of the day to make America, if not the rest of the world, open its eyes to the dangers of excessive drinking. Unfortunately the abstention of the few (who probably loathed the taste of alcohol anyway) was not sufficient to quench the thirst of those who had become accustomed to taking the occasional tipple. The ideals of the prohibitionists were confounded by the organizers of a rabbit-warren of 'speak-easys' who understood and capitalized upon the frailties of their fellows. Not surprisingly, since bars and bottles were legally banned from the American scene, most of the postcards reflected anti-drink support—even though many of the themes tried to lift the spirits with dryish humor. Bamforth and Company, Holmfirth, Yorkshire, England, published a large variety of prohibition comic cards from their New York and Chicago branches.

Staid sets of Temperance Post Cards were published by the Scholl Printing Company, Chillicothe, Ohio, and the Shaw Publishing Company, Grand Rapids, Michigan. Members of the Anti-Saloon League and the Women's Christian Temperance Movement were behind many of the card publications. Two cards illustrated here are good examples of the type of prohibition postcard seen in the postcard racks across the United States and Canada during those dry, mirthless years. The first card (Fig. 90) drawn by V. Colby, published by Muir & Co., Chicago, was copyrighted in 1911—a far-sighted warning of what was to come. The Canadian example (Fig. 91) is one of a set of 'Banish the Bar' cards, each with the patriotism of a large flag surrounding sickly, sentimental verses, and the inscription: 'For Loved Ones, Home and Native Land'. But cautionary tales in prose and verse intoned with puritanical rectitude rarely achieve the purpose of stopping people from doing what they want to do!

Public elation was stimulated in 1909 when the news came that an expedition to the North Pole had been successful. To add to the excitement this tremendous achievement was tinged with doubt about who had actually reached the goal first. Was it Pennsylvanian explorer Robert Edwin Peary, or was it Dr Frederick A. Cook, who had been a surgeon on one of Peary's earlier expeditions? Controversy swayed to and fro in the newspapers. As it was well known that Commander Peary had already made several attempts to reach the Pole, it was generally thought that if anyone could attain the ultimate objective, it would be him. Then it was headlined in the *New York Times* on September 2 1909, 'Cook Reports he has Found the North Pole', a feat which was alleged to have been accomplished over a year previously on April

I AM FOR PROHIBITION!

Copyright, 1911, V. C.

Fig. 90 'I am for Prohibition' drawn by V. Colby and published by Muir & Co., Chicago.

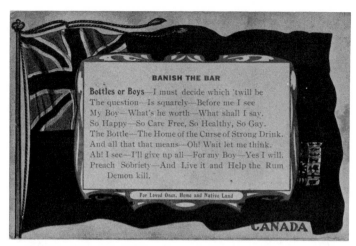

Fig. 91 'Banish the Bar' card. Private postcard published in Canada.

21 1908. Five days later came the world-shattering news, 'Peary Discovers the North Pole after Eight Trials in 23 years'. This was followed by the quotation of the cable the *New York Times* had received from Labrador:

> 'I have the Pole, April 6th. Expect arrive Chateau Bay September 7th. Secure control wire for me there and arrange expedite transmission big story. PEARY.'

Although the National Geographic Society accepted as the truth Peary's claim that he sailed to Cape Sheridan in the *Roosevelt* and then completed his journey to the Pole by sledge, Dr Cook's claim was not entirely discounted by the American public. Whatever the truth, and most present-day reference books support the authenticity of Peary's claim, the world's card publishers had a field day! Most of them were adroit enough to avoid taking sides; Dr Cook was shown with his schooner the *John R. Bradley*, Commander Peary with his steamer the *Roosevelt;* Raphael Tuck and Sons Ltd gave both explorers equal credit by commissioning Italian artist Albert Operti to paint their portraits for inclusion in their Oilette range; Kawin and Company (Chicago) produced a set of fifty photoviews of both expeditions, and inevitably there were the series of cartoons and other funnies to bring home the humor of the situation. Figs. 92 and 93 show two non-American versions of the Cook and Peary drama. Rotary Photographic series No. 7179C is a fine example of the kind of circumspection shown by publishers, and the German card originally printed in two shades of blue is typical of the humor which Cook and Peary had to put up with!

[87]

Fig. 92 Real photocard published by the Rotary Photographic Co., London, of Dr Cook and Commander Peary.

Fig. 93 German humor card describing the Cook and Peary North Pole controversy. From Robert Woodall's collection.

[88]

Both of these cards come from Robert Woodall's superb Arctic collection of postal interest. Without doubt, however, the most coveted of the Peary postcards must be the set of three cards carried aboard the SS *Roosevelt*. Card No. 1 has a picture of President Roosevelt to the left of the statement (under the general heading 'S.S. ROOSEVELT North Pole Discovery Expedition, Commander Capt. Peary, 1908'):

> 'This Post Card was posted at New York on the occasion of the "Roosevelt" leaving for the Arctic Regions in quest of the North Pole. It forms the first of a series of three.'

Beside a picture of one of the warships of Peary's opponents, Card No. 2 says:

> 'This Post Card was posted at the last port of call made by the "Roosevelt" before finally leaving civilization in the quest of the long sought for North Pole. It is the second of a series of three.'

The final card shows a view of SS *Roosevelt*—'Launched March 23, 1905 —Length: 184 feet; breadth 35 feet; Tonnage 614 tons'—and tells that:

> 'This Post Card was posted at the first port of call on the return of the "Roosevelt" from the Arctic Regions after being carried to 82.30N.'

(The degrees are handwritten.) It is the last of a series of three.

At the bottom right of each card is printed 'Cowney 111' (presumably the name of the publisher). It is not known how many of these sets were carried on board or how many are still in existence today, but Robert Woodall possesses an example of the final card in the series postmarked 'Coastal T.P.O. North, Newfoundland, September 12 1909'. There are many specialist collectors of Arctic material in the worlds of philately and deltiology, and in the American-produced specialist magazine *Ice Cap News* (published bi-monthly) there are some splendid items illustrated. This publication is the organ of the American Society of Polar Philatelists, and kindred spirits to its aims and objects should contact Shirley Jacobson, 4300 West Dempster, Skokie, Illinois, for further information regarding both the magazine and the Society.

During that first decade of the new twentieth century the world was already beginning to 'contract'; the blue-prints for high speed travel were at the outline stage on the drawing boards of go-ahead men whose inner vision had glimpsed a glittering and dramatic future for aviation. Today, real photocards of early flying-machines, aviators and the enthralment captured at air meets are priced at a premium, especially if any of them can boast postmarks of aero-philatelic interest!

Following the first international aviation meet at Rheims, France, during the last week in August 1909, the United States held a similar event at Dominquez Field, Compton, California, in January 1910. This was the start of a series of competitive air events to be held in the United States. From September 3 to 13 1910 the Harvard-Boston Flying Meet thrilled and enchanted the *avant garde* of the aviation world with the first American-British contest. Well over fifty postcards were published to commemorate this event, many of them by Aram, Boston, and others published by the Federal Engraving Company. All were photocards of the pilots with or without their aeroplanes. American flyers included famous names such as Walter Brookins, Glen Curtiss, Clifford Harman, Ralph Johnstone, and Ralph Willard. The English team had Claud Graham-White, A. V. Roe, and T. O. M. Sopwith among its representation. The following month another international air meet took place at Belmont Park on Long Island, New York. In the summer of the next year in August 1911 one of the largest air spectaculars, the International Aviation Meet, was held in Chicago, where prizes for aerobatics and air-races were contended for by Blériot monoplanes, a Curtiss hydroplane, and the bi-planes of Curtiss, Frisbie, McCurdy, Wright, and Wright-Farman.

Whatever the name chosen to describe the changing scenes, fashion, excitements, dramas, disasters, achievements, and events of more localized importance, whether it be memorabilia or social history, there was plenty of grist for the postcard mills of publishers to turn into visual memories of the days when cards were avidly collected. Now, with just as much eagerness, modern deltiologists and historians have

Fig. 94 Modern card—one of the Faga limited editions illustrating the conquest of the Atlantic.

[90]

Fig. 95 Quickly published by Veldale Limited of Kidderminster, England, a card to commemorate the release of the American Hostages who were held in Iran for 444 days. The 52 Americans were released on January 20 1981 as power passed from President Carter to President Reagan. This black and white card has the yellow ribbon printed in color, thus turning the American symbol of remembrance into a reminder of the time when much of the world shared in American rejoicing.

learned to prize those bygone issues. For not only was the postcard itself in its infancy, but discoveries of all manner of inventions, gadgetries and gimmicks were beginning to unfold to arrest the attention of a wide-eyed public. For those who have not yet joined the sophisticates who have been touched with deadening cynicism for modern wonders, there are plenty of cards to be found that illustrate the marvels of the space age and other technologies that border on the fantastic. Certainly, in the United States, there are many deltiologists who have shown the wit and the foresight to gather into their albums the pride and the glory of the postcards to illustrate the conquering by their countrymen of the Moon—a happening which must rate as the Number One accomplishment of all time, not only in the United States but also acknowledged as such by the rest of the world.

7

GREETINGS AND POSTCARDS OF VIRTUE

If satisfying the public taste for view cards was the main source of cake to keep the postcard publishers happy, then the greetings card part of their industry provided a profitable glitter of frosting on the top. In the United States, festive occasions for 'dressing up' the cake have been more frequently celebrated than in most other places. While postcards were published in the United Kingdom for Christmas, Easter, birthdays, New Years, and a few issues for St Valentine's Day, America attached a lovable importance to a much longer calendar of events. From New Year's Day to Christmas (excepting a lull between celebrating Independence Day and Thanksgiving) there was a constant bustle of postcard activity on the greetings front.

Remembering Lincoln's birthday had long been included in the postcard program, but for the celebration of his centennial on February 12 1909 there was a splendid choice of souvenir cards. Closely connected with recollections of the Civil War, many of the Centennial cards featured the Saint Gaudens and Emancipation statues, Lincoln's meeting with Grant, scenes of his inauguration, and quotations of his Gettysburg address. Raphael Tuck and Sons Ltd issued only one set of six cards, series No. 155, in recognition of this important occasion—which is strange when it is known that at least four sets exist to honor the birthday of Washington. E. Nash, a prolific publisher of early American greetings cards, published several colorful sets of Lincoln centennials bedecked with the Stars and Stripes, eagle and shield. M. W. Taggart (New York) and Paul Finkenrath (Berlin) were also among leading publishers of important Lincoln Centennial cards. An especially beautiful example of such cards was illustrated in color (Plate 190) in the book *Collecting Postcards in Colour 1894–1914*, where an inset oval portrait of Lincoln is surrounded by patriotic regalia against the figure of a sorrowing mother, beside which is a facsimile of the sympathy letter written to her by Lincoln, and underneath are the words:

'"A Man of Sorrow Acquainted with Grief"
Ever conscientiously struggling for right and in the midst of the perplexities of formidable responsibilities never forgetting the misfortunes of others.'

It seems that they do not grow men with the sentiments and stature of Lincoln as leaders any more!

Ten days after the commemorations of Lincoln's birthday it was time for the postcards to celebrate the birth of George Washington to be slipped through the mailboxes on February 22. A number of the Washington cards were decorated with cherries as symbols of truth as well as the emblems of American patriotism. Among the deltiological rarities to honor both Presidents Lincoln and Washington are the cards published by the Anglo-American Post Card Company in sets resembling the features of an open book; across from the fine portraits of each President appear quotations of their sayings within a rose-decorated surround. The tradition of publishing and sending such cards continues today; a recent set published by Walter H. Miller & Co., Inc., Williamsburg, Virginia, extols in a snatch of verse the virtues of the VIPs pictured on their fronts. To go with a painting by Robert Edge Pine of George Washington, a couplet of lines tells that he was:

'First in war, first in peace,
    first in the hearts of his countrymen.'

With a Joseph Siffrid Duplessis portrait of Benjamin Franklin it is learned that: 'He snatched the lightning from heaven and the scepter from tyrants'. Another modern series published by Dexter Press Inc., West Nyack, New York, furnishes a brief history of the lives of past Presidents notated on the reverse, and on the back of one of their recent cards for Lincoln's birthday he is described as 'probably the best beloved of our presidents'.

After the patriotic birthday celebrations of Presidents Lincoln and Washington comes Memorial Day, or Decoration Day as it used to be called, a day set aside for the remembrance of American servicemen who gave their lives in war. The general date for this day of quiet reflection is May 30, but in the Southern States it varies from April 26 to June 3. There are, as can be imagined, many cards to be found to perpetuate the memory of the fallen; and all depict a poignant tenderness and pride. If some betray the sort of sentiment to bring a lump to the throat, what fault can be found in that? In the words printed on one

[93]

Fig. 96 One of the New Year cards by Julia Woodworth in her 'Cupid' series, published by F. A. Owen Co., Dansville, New York.

Fig. 98 A Washington Birthday card with the Winsch back of laurel leaves drawn over double-lined squares.

Fig. 97 Embossed Valentine Greetings published by Stecher Litho Company Rochester, New York.

Fig. 99 Flag series No. 4 published anonymously for 'Memorial Day'.

of the cards published by the International Art Publishing Company, New York:

'Today the thronging millions troop
  Where floats that standard in their view,
And ours, dear Flag, the joy to stand
  Beneath thee loyal to our Land.'

Raphael Tuck and Sons Ltd published several 'Decoration Day' sets, but it must be said that in an obvious anxiety to choose the right words to suit the occasion there emerged an uncharacteristic clumsiness when quite beautiful designs were marred by offerings like 'In glory underneath the sod, slumber our heroes today', or 'It is little we can do to show our love for you, O warriors blest'. Whatever happened to all those writers of prose and verse—brilliant enough to win prizes in the 'Tuck Literary Competitions'?

In sharp contrast to the gentleness of Memorial Day postcard meditations are the cards next in the date line for a swell of patriotic emotions. Independence Day was given as much of the full razzle-dazzle treatment on postcards as anywhere else. Fourth of July cards burgeoned out with the gaiety of gardens filled with the scented fruits and flowers of sun-drenched summers. This was the day (as it still is) when every American busts out all over with the sheer joy of being American. Like Christmas, the day commemorating American Independence is a day when expansive generosity is shown to every neighbor; a day of elation when grudges and greeds are pushed aside until the next day, when just like the aftermath of Christmas euphoria the greeds and grudges are even more sharply remembered. The glory of Uncle Sam, the charm of Miss Liberty, the loyalty and pride of Americans protecting the insignias of freedoms hard earned and proudly won were the popularly traditional themes to mark the anniversary of the day when the United States of American won the battle for freedom and had conferred upon her the title of 'God's Own Country'. The United States who offered hope and a home to so many races of different creeds, colors and customs had, and still has, good cause to celebrate the glories of the Fourth of July. Raphael Tuck and Sons Ltd enriched the 'Independence Day' postcard scene by issuing a couple of sets of twelve cards in each from cheerful patriotic and firecracker embellishments to Revolutionary scenes and children bursting out of gift-wrappings waving aloft miniature flags. The Ullman Manufacturing Company commissioned Bernhardt Wall to design a series to include sketches of Uncle Sam and 'Miss Independence'. The Fred C. Lounsbury Co. struck a more serious note by publishing a set entitled 'Memories of the War of Independence', copyrighted 1907. But most of the Fourth July cards were typified by the use of firecracker designs and defiantly patriotic motifs.

During the first half of every year dispersed between the postcard parades of patriotism were the fixed days for honoring the days of Saints Valentine and Patrick. February the fourteenth was the day when every pretty girl expected as her right a full complement of postcard offerings from a small brigade of secret (and some not so secret) admirers. A bright profusion of colored and often embossed themes of hearts and flowers and sometimes hilariously comical cards were designed and produced every year by artists and postcard publishers who knew instinctively how a young man's fancy might be captured—and often was! The festival of St Valentine, patron saint of lovers, originated when Valentinus, a Roman bishop of the early Christian Church, was clubbed to death on February 14, the eve of the start of the celebration of Lupercalia. The custom in those far away days was to sacrifice goats and a dog and for the priests to run around the city with goatskin thongs—from which a blow to a woman was believed to cure her from sterility, a fertility magic which also had the combined charm of protection against wolves. After the martyrdom of St Valentine the more lascivious behaviour connected with the Lupercalia gradually began to die out and was gently restored into a habit of offering inoffensive gifts to wives and girlfriends, and, of course, the sending of Valentine cards. However, shades of the old Lupercalia are revealed when the term 'wolf' is used by women to describe the unwelcome advances of lecherous males!

Shamrocks, pretty Irish colleens, Irish harps, piglets cavorting among four-leaf clovers and 'raising a glass to "Dear Old Ireland"' were among the favorite designs on postcards to entice the traffic in cards for St Patrick's Day, March 17. Raphael Tuck and Sons Ltd published a dozen or so sets to delight the Irish population, especially the Irish-Americans. 'To Erin's Daughter', series No. 117, is a scarce and charming set drawn by American artist Cyrus Durand Chapman, accompanied by toasts such as:

'Here' a toast in th' rosy cup
  To Swatehearts far acrost th' sea,
    Wid wine av hope
      We'll fill it up,
  An' drink to days that yet may be.'

'The Erin Go Bragh' and 'The Emerald Isle' series are also animated with Irish good humor, and there are plenty of 'The top o' the Mornin' to ye' type of phrases to be seen in the Tuck's 'St Patrick's Day' sets. M. W. Taggart, New York, published a set of musical scores in 1908 of six Irish songs; John Winsch, another very popular New York

[96]

*Fig. 100   Series No. 446 of 6 designs of Mother's Day
cards. Anonymously published in the USA.*

publisher, produced several attractive sets of pretty colleens drawn by
S. L. Schmucker, and there were many Irish cards attributed to Frances
Brundage published by the Samuel Cupples Envelope Company, Saint
Louis, and to Ellen Clapsaddle in sets produced by International Art
Publishing Co.

Easter postcards made full use of spring-flower themes and baby-
bunnies and chicks bursting out of egg-shells; and, of course, there
were many beautifully colored and embossed crosses and angels
triumphantly proclaiming the miracle of the Resurrection. A small
issue of greetings cards appeared to honor Mothers' Day on May 10,
and during the years of World War I there were also attempts to popularize postcards to celebrate a similar day set aside for honoring
Fathers—and even a Parents' Day. But although several decades later
Fathers managed to circulate around the postcard orbit, the idea for a
joint Parents' Day has not so far caught on.

After the climax of National Greetings days on Fourth July, there
was a lull in the postcard greetings market (apart from the hardy
perennial habit of sending family birthday cards) until the green shades
of summer turned to russet and gold to welcome the fall. Then came the
anticipation of hollowing out the pumpkins to make jack-o'-lanterns
for Hallowe'en parties. Jack-o'-lanterns, witches, black cats, red
devils, and all kinds of spooky-looking creatures were the familiars to
decorate a mass of Hallowe'en postcards every year. Postcard publishers had a lot of fun with the production of these; again Raphael
Tuck and Sons Ltd produced a dozen or so different sets over the years;

Fig. 101 All-Hallow-E'en Carnival card for Albany, New York, published 1905 by Ben V. Smith and the Albany Art Union.

Fig. 102 A Julia Woodworth 'Cupid' card in the Thanksgiving series published by F. A. Owen Co., Danville, New York.

Fig. 104 One of the desirable Whitney made cards from Worcester, Massachusetts, for Thanksgiving Day.

Fig. 103 Anonymously published lightly embossed card for Thanksgiving.

John Winsch, New York, issued many sets of the traditionally eery antics of ghosts and goblins, witches on broomsticks, and an especially notable set designed by Jason Freixas showing children carrying jack-o'-lanterns; Paul Finkenrath (Berlin) also depicted children enjoying the fun of Hallowe'en.

After the spooks and witches had been chased away for another year, preparations were well ahead for the last major American celebration before the rush for Christmas cards began. The American Thanksgiving Day on the fourth Thursday in November (combined as it was with the Christmas schedule for card producing) made this time of the year especially hectic for postcard publishers. In the early days of the postcard era there was not the forward planning that exists today. As a result the absence of stock-piling cards several months ahead of an event gave scope for more up-to-date themes of topicality; not that the themes for Thanksgiving and Christmas have changed much over the years. There is still a predominant show of Pilgrims simply dressed in Quaker style, scenes of a successful harvest, and the inevitable showing of turkeys, either full feathered and fan-tailed or resting in the place of honor on the tables of the traditional Thanksgiving dinners. John Winsch (New York) also produced sets of cards to feature serene scenes of Colonial life, and beautiful sets of portraits drawn by S. Schmucker of early Indian and Puritan ladies. As predictable as the sight of turkeys seen on Thanksgiving cards, there were over a dozen different sets published by Raphael Tuck and Sons Ltd, with designs from the very simple to the embossed elaborate. Thanksgiving was the time when all the American postcard publishers could be reckoned on to give of their best. Philip Sander produced several notable series including scenes of the *Mayflower* in Plymouth harbor and most had strong patriotic themes like Uncle Sam and Miss Liberty dining at a Thanksgiving table colorfully draped with the American flag. E. Nash, as well as publishing the recognized themes of nuts and fruits and fatted turkeys, brought home the true meaning of thankfulness by showing a small child, hands folded and eyes closed in prayer as grace was being said at the Thanksgiving dinner.

Choosing from the immense choice of designs to decorate the Christmas postcard must have been among the more pleasurable toils of the postcard publishers. Frosted snow scenes sparkled around vivid red center-pieces of poinsettias, birds perched amid the holly and mistletoe beneath clusters of Christmas bells, warmly clad children played in the snow, and benevolent Santas with or without reindeer and sleighs sped merrily on their joy-making missions. Themes such as these were always among the most favorite with the card-buying public. But Christmas was the time when postcards could best be elaborated into

Merry Christmas!

MR. S. CLAUS

U.S. MAIL

DEAR SANTA PLESE SEND ME A NEW PAIR OF WINGS OR ELSE A AEROPLANE YOURS TRULY CUPID

JULIA WOODWORTH CUPID CARDS · CHRISTMAS SERIES

947

Fig. 105 Card from F.A.Owen Co. Christmas Cupid series by Julia Wood-worth.

interesting novelties—like the instalment idea copyrighted by Franz Huld of New York. On the lines of sets called 'composite' by Europeans, instalment cards came in sets of four and the idea was for one card to be sent each day of the four days preceding Christmas Day. Huld's 'Puzzle' series No. 9a–9d builds up into a picture of Santa Claus; the card showing his boots marked 9a was sent first, thus inducing an additional flurry of anticipation until the last card (9d) arrived to reveal his face and the contents of his sack of toys. Series 10 of the Huld's Puzzle cards shows a decorated tree and starts in the more conventional way from top to bottom. Later on Franz Huld adapted this novelty to an Easter theme depicting a large Easter Bunny in series No. 14.

Scenes of snow-clad cottages and churches with their windows cut-out and sophisticated transparencies like the Meteor types of decorated Christmas trees which disclosed angels and children opening presents, and the glow from the cut-out windows when held-to-light, were ever popular. So was the essentially American idea of incorporating a folded type greeting on the front of a postcard with a tiny clip or removable seal to keep the card intact for posting without an envelope. Another novelty prevalent at Christmas time was not so much an invention of postcard publishers but more a 'do-it-yourself' idea: with the aid of a special steel pen and tinsel glue, and an array of different colored

Fig. 106 Delightful Christmas greetings card by Pauli Ebner published by Marcus Munk (M.M. Vienne), No. 779.

tinsels, messages could be written and outlines of a design traced on almost any of the commercial cards purchased. Most of these efforts were not expertly executed and those found by today's deltiologists are generally disregarded as 'damaged' cards.

Although Christmas is an important religious festival, there were not many cards depicting Nativity scenes, but those that were found were usually superbly colored and often gilded and embossed. Paul Finkenrath, Berlin, a master publisher of religious themes, published several sets to illustrate the most celebrated birthday of all.

Other opportunities to send a greetings card to friends (apart from individual birthdays) were not as well marked on postcards. The first Monday in September, for example, is set aside as a legal holiday in the United States in honor of Labor. Officially recognized by Congress in 1894, Labor Day somehow failed to attract the imagination of card publishers. From the deltiologist's viewpoint this lethargy is all to the good, for Labor Day postcards are scarce, and as scarcity is a keyword in the vocabulary of collectors these cards have a special magnetism.

Birth announcement postcards enjoyed a limited span of popularity with storks bearing a variety of congratulatory greetings. At the other end of the scale, there were a few sympathy postcards offering condolences in times of bereavement. There were also the Rally Day cards, similar in intent to the Reward cards which were issued in the United Kingdom to encourage regular attendance at Sunday School. The pictures on these cards were not especially inspiring to the young. As far as collecting the huge assortment of greetings cards is concerned the

[101]

Fig. 107   Birthday card drawn by Pauli Ebner for the Alpha Publishing Co., London.

Fig. 108   Horoscope reading card for 18-23 May—to alert all Geminis. Published by the Exhibit Sup. Co., Chicago, early 1920s.

Fig. 109   One of the examples of the Virtue cards by Mailick for 'Hope'.

range is practically infinite, making this category of deltiology an excellent starting point for beginners on the postcard trail. A heartening sight to cheer the faint-hearted is the collection of a young American student who started a 'Greetings of the World' collection in the late 1970s and has now filled almost a dozen albums each holding 400 cards without duplicating a card once! Across the ocean in the United Kingdom there are several youngsters in their third year at University who are well on their way to achieving a similar goal. Such is the enthusiasm among students for postcard collecting that much of their leisure is spent on researching the subject.

As so many of the occasions for sending a greetings card are related to religious festivals, even if the designs on postcards rarely dwell on the spiritual significance of Easter, Thanksgiving, and Christmas (although the eminently collectable cards issued to celebrate the Jewish New Year are usually a different matter), it is fitting to describe some of the cards in this chapter which American deltiologists have aptly put under the heading of 'Virtue'.

Whereas building enormous collections of exterior and interior views of churches takes no time at all, gathering in the more beautiful cards designed to pierce the conscience is not such an easy pastime—at least, not as easy now as it was two or three years back. This is not to say that the deltiologists who have suddenly 'discovered' the lovely sets of The Lord's Prayer, The Ten Commandments and the gilded renderings of cards like the Mailick virtues have suddenly 'seen the light' to become models of pious virtue themselves. Whether the rock musicals *Godspell* and *Jesus Christ Superstar* have had anything to do with the upsurge of interest in cards with definite religious themes is not known, but certainly since the success of these two shows there has been a marked increase in demand. (No less so has been the demand from the Catholic shops in the UK for cards of the prayer of St Francis, ever since Prime Minister Mrs Margaret Thatcher quoted it from the entrance of Number Ten Downing Street, before taking up residence there on May 4 1979!)

First in line of interest are the virtues Faith, Hope, Charity, Patience, Purity and Innocence; the most famous sets of which were drawn by Mailick and published by G.B. Co. To endorse the earlier popularity of these, many of the important postcard publishers such as Giesen Bros., the Illustrated Post Card Company, the International Art Company, M. T. Sheahan (who also published a fine line in virtuous Mottoes), the Rotograph Company, Paul Finkenrath, the Philco Company and Raphael Tuck and Sons Ltd followed suit. Next comes the search for cards that show angels hovering in the background—preferably with the words 'The Guardian Angel' clearly printed on the front of pictures

Fig. 110 The IVth Commandment from the set No. 163P of 'The Ten Commandments' published by Raphael Tuck & Sons Ltd.

of children being steered back from the horrific dangers they are toddling towards!

From such virtuous and angelic beginnings, progress has now travelled in the direction which prompts the question to dealers: 'Have you a set of The Ten Commandments and/or The Lord's Prayer?' Mostly the answer is a glum shake of the head, for nowadays such sets are only obtainable in the auction room where they usually fetch extraordinarily high prices! Raphael Tuck and Sons Ltd published a couple of sets of the Commandments, No. 163P for Protestants and No. 163C for Catholics; Paul Finkenrath (Berlin) published an equally scarce set; M. W. Taggart (New York) and the T. Rose Company each issued sets on a more plentiful scale, and there were other sets printed in Germany but anonymously published. Complete sets of The Lord's Prayer, comprising eight cards in each, are no easier to find. Paul Finkenrath issued several sets with different pictures to interpret the meaning; and many were published in translations of French and German as well as English. An all-American version of the PFB set No. 7064 was reproduced in clear bright colors and lightly embossed. Philco published a set with a gelatin coating that cracks with too much handling, and Philip Sander came up with a blue bordered version surrounding American scenes in 1908.

Colorful sets of cards recounting stories from both the Old and New Testaments were also favored by early postcard collectors, and are sought after now by their successors; as are the sets to describe the Stations of the Cross. Especially beautiful are the reproductions of Biblical scenes painted by the Old Masters published by Stengel (Dresden) and E. Sborgi (Florence). A particularly fine card in the illuminated style so much favored by E. Sborgi was issued as a limited edition in aid of the Calabrian Fund during the reign of Pope Pius X. Quite clearly from the leaflet distributed with the special 'Papal Post Card', whoever was responsible for marketing these cards was astutely aware of the craze for collecting. Since then, the Vatican has lost none of this awareness of the importance of the picture postcards, for there have been countless cards published showing the likenesses of successive Pontiffs—but few will be more consistently collectable than those issued of Pope John Paul II, especially those which were issued to honor his visits to the United States and Ireland in 1979.

THE HEART OF AMERICAN DELTIOLOGY

In all collecting fields there are the divisions of interest between the purist collector who collects for pleasure and very often has a conscience about the sort of stuff that should be set aside in the interests of posterity, and the dealer who has a living to earn. In the deltiological and philatelic worlds there is a kind of love-hate relationship between collector and dealer; and this is more marked in the younger world of postcards than in the more venerable one of stamps and postmarks. Nothing upsets deltiologists more than the parade of postcard-priced catalogues compiled by dealers who appear to be more concerned with outdoing their rivals by producing price guides that bear no relation to the more conservative views of ordinary collectors. Most of these catalogues used to appear annually at around the same time, and each with their vastly differing values were guaranteed to raise the blood pressure of collectors who were masochistically disposed to exercising this annual form of flagellation by being first in the queue to acquire the latest editions of aggravation.

Fortunately, in the United States, an antidote against the hysteria of postcard-cataloguitis is available upon application to any of the many Postcard Clubs to have been established across the States. Based on the good humor and good will of their memberships, it is in these clubs where the heart of American deltiology beats with vigorous strength. The clubs to be first off the mark after the ending of World War 2 were those based in Connecticut and New York. A delightfully happy photocard illustrated in Fig. 111 shows the members of the Metropolitan Post Card Collectors Club at their Third Annual Exhibition, New York City, on December 5 1952. There are now many, many more clubs instituted in America to have stemmed from early pioneer examples; examples to have been followed by postcard devotees in the United Kingdom by the

Fig. 111   Real photocard of members of the Metropolitan Post Card Collectors Club New York City, 1952.

early 1960s, and then in many other parts of the world.

Even so, postcard clubs in America are much more advanced in their organization. Meetings are mostly run in the same way as philatelic societies and are usually held every month at a given time at a regular meeting place. (One club in the UK to follow this successful formula is the Norfolk Postcard Club, East Anglia, England.) However, activities do not begin and end with dates of meetings for members' diaries. There are many extra events going on throughout the year, special club bourses, the staging of interesting exhibitions, visits to view important collections and so on. With a thoughtful eye always open for collectable cards of the future, modern cards are welcomed rather than disdained—even to the extent of many of the clubs producing cards of their own. The American interest in present-day cards sums up the dedication and foresight of club involvement in the hobby and illustrates that at least one very important section of the postcard-collecting world understands the essence and aims of deltiology in its purest form. While acknowledging that antique postcards have become investment propositions, the members of American Postcard Clubs are equally quick to acknowledge that, if the hobby is to continue, a healthy regard must be paid to the offerings from the modern postcard racks. They find nothing complicated either about following the simple rules laid down by their ancestors who started the craze in the first place, i.e. to collect what is most fancied at the ground-floor price of a few cents, and let the dollars look after themselves later on! In the dollars-for-tomorrow category comes any modern card to reflect the

Fig. 113   A 1912 A. M. Davis postcard message card.

Fig. 112   Publicity card for the Garden State and Metropolitan Post Card Clubs, a Mucha reproduction dated 1966.

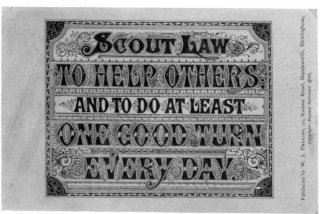

Fig. 114   The Scout Law published by W. J. Parkins, Birmingham, England. From John and Doreen Powell's collection.

Fig. 115   Scouting card drawn by Ernest Ibbetson, published by C. W. Faulkner & Co. Ltd, London, from series 970.

times and dramas of today. For this reason, a small selection of modern cards has been included in this chapter and in the color section as well as one or two of those that have been published for and by postcard clubs.

While regular news bulletins are usually sent out to members of each club, it is not always easy for the newcomer to deltiology to discover the whereabouts of the nearest venue of experts. Surely the ideal introduction to any leisure pursuit is to be able to contact one or two of the veterans in the field—if only out of curiosity in the first place! So for readers who would like to learn more about postcards (hopefully with the view of pursuing more than an idle interest) a list of American Post Card Clubs is given below; and for American deltiologists who might feel it an advantage to be in closer touch with their British fellows there is also a list of British clubs.

No newcomer to the fascination of collecting postcards can do better than to make his first contact through one of the recognized clubs; for in the world of collecting traditional collectables the word 'collector' is usually considered to be synonymous with 'connoisseur', and there are plenty of those to be found at the heart of American deltiology. Such hearts beat warm for the young, too, when it is learned of campaigns like the one launched by Ruth Weimer of the Central New York Postcard Club who is trying to persuade the national office of the Boy Scouts to include collecting postcards in the list of activities and hobbies that earn badges of merit. Stamp and coin collecting are already on the list, so why not deltiology? No doubt, since her campaign started, Ruth Weimer has been responsible for inducing deltiologists to write to the national address, Boy Scouts of America, New Brunswick, New Jersey 08902, offering assistance to Scouts, and free membership to clubs while they are working for a deltiology badge of merit.

American Postcard Clubs

Alaska Collectors Club, Don S. Dimpsey, P.O. Box 579, Sumner WA 98390

Angels Flight Postcard Club, 2027 Appleton Street, 5 Long Beach, California 90803

Bay State Postcard Club, Boston, Massachusetts, Mrs Anne Miller, Box 344, Lexington, MA 02173

Birmingham Picture Postcard Club, Mrs J. W. Craig, 1449 Ridge Road, Homewood, AL 35209

Black Hawk Postcard Club, Aretta Wetzel, 1325-45 St., Rock Island IL 61201

Fig. 116 'He was bred in old Kentucky' and what a beauty he must have been in 1905!

Fig. 117 The Ladies' Horse Show, Durlands, April 27 1910. A nice bit of dressage—despite doggy interruptions!

Fig. 119 From Raphael Tuck & Sons Ltd. 'Connoisseur' series No. 2568.

Fig. 118 From series No. 895 published by Alfred Stiebel & Co., London.

Capitol Beltway Postcard Club, D.C. area, C. R. Collins, 19 Empire Place, Greenbelt, MD 20770

Cedar-loo Postcard Club, Mary Jensen, 1516 Orchard Drive, Cedar Falls, IA 50613

Cedar Rapids Postcard Club, Vivian Rinaberger, 4548 Fairland Drive, N.E., Cedar Rapids IA 52402

Central New York Postcard Club, Ruth R. Weimer, RD 2-Box 173, Route 31, Canastota, New York 13032

Cheerio Postcard Club, Peggy Smith, Arnolds Park, IA 51331

Connecticut Postcard Club, Mrs W. Robinson, 15 Ridgewood Road, Rowayton, CT 06853

Cowtown Postcard Club, Box 3105, Fort Worth, Texas 76105

Denver Postcard Club, 955 Eudora Street, Denver, CO 80220

Evanston Postcard Club, Nick Kalman, 1070 Tower Road, Winetka, IL 60093

Garden State Postcard Collectors Club, Dolores Kirchgessner, P.O. Box 1005, Secaucus, N.J. 07094

Gateway Postcard Club, Saint Louis, P.O. Box 1082, St. Ann, MO 63074

Golden Gate Postcard Club, San Francisco, Mildred Hopson, 440 Moffett Boulevard, SP.65, Mountain View CA 94043

Great South Bay Postcard Club, Long Island, New York, Dorothy Miller, 29 Wilson Drive, Babylon, New York 11702

Greater Houston Postcard Society, Mrs Leila Regan, 4007 Coleridge, Houston, TX 77005

Half Moon Postcard Club, Agnes Cavalari, R.D.2. Bethlehem Road, New Windsor, New York 12550

Hawkeye Postcard Club, Brad Snodgrass, 405 E. Salem, Indianola, IA 50125

Heart of Ohio Postcard Club, Betty Sidle, Rt.2, 444 Heather Lane, Powell, OH 43065

Homewood-Flossmoor Postcard Club, Leslie Lawitz, 18820 Highland Avenue, Homewood, IL 60430

Houston Postcard Club, Mrs Kathryn Parker, 10803 Hunters Forest, Houston, Texas 77024

Indianapolis Postcard Club, Fred G. Bachmann, 2623 Andy Drive, Indianapolis, IN 46229

Johnny Appleseed Postcard Club, P.O. Box 2257, Mansfield, Ohio 44905

Katterskill Kardiacs Postcard Club, Mariam Posner, 277 Millers Lane, Ext. Kingston, NY 12401

Fig. 120 'The Symbols of Liberty' Bi-Centennial American Revolution 1776–1976 card published by the South Jersey Post Card Club.

Fig. 121 The Plaza, New York — one of the famous Hilton Hotels.

Fig. 122 Avid deltiologist Jocelyn D. Decker, who is now the secretary of the Webfooter Club, featured on a postcard.

Lone Star Postcard Collectors Club, Floy Case, 2300 Lincoln, Fort Worth, TX 76106

Maple City Postcard Club, Miss Alice Reed, MCPCC, P.O. Box 644, Elkhart, IN 46515

The Marin Postcard Club, George Epperson, 164 Du Bois, San Rafael, California 94901

Metropolitan Postcard Collectors Club, New York City, Rose Shriffrin, 16-08 212th Street, Bayside, New York 11360

Milwaukee Postcard Collectors Club, Evelyn Tiedemann, 2115 So. 15th Pl. Milwaukee, WI 53215

Monumental Postcard Club of Maryland, Mrs Peggy Bower, 2902 Ontario Avenue, Baltimore, MD 21234

Morlattan Postcard Club, PA, Louise Stanley, 3 West Broad Street, Shillinton, PA 19607

North Georgia Postcard Club, Sandi Pence, 122 Fernbanks Ct, Athens, GA 30610

Pacific Northwest Postcard Club, Betty Allen, 1300 N. Alder, Ellensburg, WA 98926

The Pine Tree Postcard Club, Jon Stokes, 30 Sanborn St., Portland, Maine 04103

Postcard Collectors Club of Buffalo, New York, Louise Phillips, 165 Bickford Avenue, Buffalo, NY 14215

Postcard History Society, Roy Cox, Box 3610, Baltimore, MD 21214

Postcard Pals, Local Iowa Club, Mrs Thomas Weiland, 2324 Maplewood Drive, Rt.5, Dubuque, IA 52001

Rhode Island Postcard Club, Evelyn Marshall, 37 Ryder Avenue, 2, Cranston, RI 02920

The Santa Monica Postcard Club, Adrian Verburg, 1112-11th St., Santa Monica, California 90403

South Jersey Postcard Club, Gloria Downes, 100 Champlain Avenue, Wilm., DE 19804

The Southwestern Michigan Postcard Collectors' Exchange Club, Louise B. Northam, 1833 Waite Avenue, Kalamazoo, Michigan 49008

Sunshine Postcard Club, Dorothy Laughlin, 711 S/W, 73rd Avenue, Miami, Florida 33144

Tarheel Postcard Club, Roberta Griener, 1614 Helmwood Drive, Greensboro, NC 27410

Tropical Postcard Club, Judy Ripple, P.O. Box 22307, Fort Lauderdale, FL 33335

AP - H

Twin City Postcard Club, Box 4176, St. Paul, MN 55104

The Upstate Postcard Club, Dorothy Baron, 1832 Fiero Avenue, Schenectady, NY 12303

Washington Crossing Card Collectors' Club, Secretary WC4, P.O. Box 39, Washington Crossing, PA 18977

Webfooter Postcard Club, Jocelyn Decker, P.O. Box 843, Albany, Oregon, 97321

Western New York Postcard Club, Mrs Nancy Williams, 3520 Atlantic Avenue, Penfield, New York 14526

Western Reserve Postcard Society, Betty Toth, 13538 Shady Oak Boulevard, Garfield Hts., Ohio, 44125

Wichita Postcard Club, Hal Ottaway, Box 18282, Wichita, Kansas 67218

Wilmington Postcard Club, Jo Newcomer, 4 Fallon Avenue, Wilmington DE 19804

Windy City Postcard Club, Membership Secretary, WCPCC, Box 8118, Chicago IL 60680

Wolverine Postcard Club, Laura N. Goldberg, 1313 E. Harry, Hazel Park, MI 48030

Mail Clubs Only

Chrome Card Collectors Club, Box 508, Bound Brook, New York 08805

Cuba International Postcard Club, Frank J. Pichardo, P.O. Box 1116, Flushing, New York 11354

Deltiologists of America, James Lowe, 3709 Gradyville Road, Newton Square, PA 19073

Equine Deltiologists of America, Debbie Curtiss, Route 2, Box 314, Yakima, WA 98902

EXPO Collectors and Historians Organization, Edward J. Orth, 1436 Killarney Avenue, Los Angeles, California 90065

Exposition Postcard Collectors Club, Hobbs Jackson, Box 116, Lafayette, AL 36862

International Railroad & Transportation Postcard Collectors Club, Robert J. Andrews, P.O. Box 6783, Providence RI 02940

New Zealand-American International Collectors Club, Daphne Litke, Box 265, Palmer, MA 01069

Organization for Collecting Covered Bridge Postcards, Ethel Snider, 7265 Amanda Northern Road, Canal Winchester, OH 43110

Postcard Club, Linda Lord, 4613 Eugene Drive, Bristol, PA 19007

Rotograph Society, Alvin Goldstein, 1625 W. 25 St., Minneapolis, MN 55405

The American Postcard Journal

Up to October 1979 just about the best of all the postcard magazines was published bi-monthly by Roy and Marilyn Nuhn of West Haven, Connecticut. For a while it was feared that deltiologists everywhere were to be denied any further issues. However, early in the 1980s Roy and Marilyn arranged for their excellent work to be continued by Donald and Sue Bodow of Syracuse, New York. Published under the new name of *Picture Postcard News* this magazine is available from: Donald M. Bodow and Sue L. Bodow, P.O. Box 20, Syracuse, New York 13201. Writing to them enclosing a *stamped addressed envelope* (which should be enclosed with any letter written to the above postcard clubs as well!) might be worth the inquiry about what they have available by way of back numbers of the *American Postcard Journal* too.

Buying and Selling Postcards

To attempt to list all the dealers in postcards across the United States would fill a book on its own; so to avoid giving offense by only listing a few and leaving out a lot, the advice is to contact Postcard Club secretaries for up-to-date information.

United Kingdom Postcard Clubs

Postcard Club of Great Britain, Mrs Drene Brennan, 34 Harper House, St James' Crescent, London SW9

Huddersfield and District Postcard Society, George Wolstenholme, 13 Westroyd Park, Mirfield, Yorkshire

Leeds Postcard Club, Mrs A. Whitelock, 9 Brentwood Grove, Leeds LS12 2DB

Lincoln Collectors' Club, T. G. Collier, 2 Wickenby Close, Fosse Estate, North Hykeham, Lincolnshire

Norfolk Postcard Club, P. J. Standley, 63 Folly Road, Wymondham, Norfolk

Bradford and District Postcard Club, A. E. Wood, 26 Front View, Shelf, Halifax, West Yorkshire

Tees Valley Collectors' Club, A. J. Lambert, 15 Glenfield Road, Darlington, Co. Durham

London Postcard Club, Mrs Joyce Cohen, 58 Sandringham Road, London NW11

North of England Postcard Club, F. A. Fletcher, 35 St Georges Terrace, East Bolden, Tyne and Wear

Study Circle for Early Numbered Tuck Postcards, Mr Tony Warr, Fairview, Ickford, Shabbington, Aylesbury, Buckinghamshire

Kent Postcard Club, Jack Smith, Pattison Farm, Aldington, Kent

Northern Ireland Postcard Club, Roy Campbell, 70 The Green, Dunmurry, Co. Antrim, Northern Ireland

The Suffolk Postcard Club, Mrs Peggy Southgate, 8 The Green, Mistley, Manningtree, Essex

Newcastle-upon-Tyne Postcard Club, Mrs M. Osborne, 26 Balmoral Terrace, South Gosforth, Newcastle-upon-Tyne

Rushden Northants Postcard Club, Mr B. C. Church, 2 Meadow Drive, Higham Ferrars, Rushden, Northants

Maidstone Postcard Club, Mrs I. Hales, 40 Hildenborough Crescent, Maidstone, Kent

Sussex Postcard Club, Mr Dave Bull, 12 The Broadway, Lancing, Sussex

Hertfordshire Postcard Club, Neil Jenkins, 113 Bramble Road, Hatfield, Hertfordshire

Canal Card Collectors' Circle, A. K. Robinson, 56 Henley Avenue, Dewsbury, West Yorkshire

Surrey Postcard Club, Simon Burke, 7 Sandfield Terrace, Guildford, Surrey

British Postcard Journals

The Postcard Monthly. A co-ordination of Reflections of a Bygone Age and Postcard Collectors Gazette. Edited by Brian and Mary Lund, 27 Walton Drive, Keyworth, Nottinghamshire

The British Postcard Magazine. Edited by Ron Griffiths, 47 Long Arrotts, Hemel Hempstead, Hertfordshire HP1 3EX.

Transy News. Edited by Harold Richardson, 27b Marchmont Road, Edinburgh EH9 1HY

Information for American visitors to Britain

Postcard Auctions. Monthly sales held at Caxton Hall by Mr Ken Lawson, MCC/SPA (extensive catalogues always include several items of USA interest). Postal bids accepted. Contact Ken Lawson at MCC/SPA, 24 Watford Road, Wembley, Middlesex.

Postcard Bourses. Held monthly at the Bloomsbury Center Hotel, and at Central Hall, Westminster, London. Organized by John H. D. Smith, IPM Promotions Ltd.

Postcard Dealers. Names and addresses are regularly advertised in postcard journals and the annual priced catalogues published by IPM Promotions Ltd and Picton's published by B.P.H. Publications, Chippenham, Wiltshire.

SOME VALUATIONS OF AMERICAN POSTCARDS

For deltiologists accustomed to travelling to different countries, shopping for postcards is a bit like touring round the supermarkets, when cards found and purchased in one country are very often found at a much cheaper price in another. The same aggravation is encountered at the postcard bourses; buy a card at one stand for a price considered to be reasonable enough—until a similar card is spotted at another for much less. The moral about it being prudent to have a good look round first is often cancelled out too; for, by the time the browsing session is over, all the good cards, no matter their price, have been snapped up by somebody else.

The business of pricing postcards has always been a prickly subject. In Europe there are many annually produced priced catalogues, and each reflect the mood of different markets based upon the experience of their compilers. It cannot be otherwise when no one can put an exact figure on the vast number of postcards to have been published; and, apart from those postcards which are known to have been limited in supply, no one can accurately answer the question of 'how scarce is scarce?', for cards that are scarce to find in one country may be quite plentiful in another. Compilers of catalogues have an awkward task to perform, and since they know there is no pleasing everybody they often receive for their pains more brickbats than bouquets. Over the year between the publication of one catalogue and another, they can only record the movements of the different postcard categories and the fluctuations of prices from the observations made by their groups of advisers—who are usually drawn from the more respected circles of experienced dealers. Priced catalogues, therefore, and valuations such as those given in this book, can only be viewed as guides to give some idea of the range between one postcard category and another, and always at the back of the mind

[117]

should the cautionary tale about the 'dips and rises' in postcard fashions be remembered. It must also be strongly mentioned that, just as prices vary in other countries, the same versatility applies to the postcards of the United States of America; and bearing in mind that a week or two is a long time in the postcard field by the time this book is published a lot could be out of date!

Private Mailing Cards with imprint Authorized by Act of Congress May 19 1898 on reverse side were existent until 1907 with their undivided backs. Prices for these early cards depend too much upon subject, publisher, artist etc for price assessments to be made on a general basis.

Viewcards in monochrome or color:	.25–$5 + for main streets
Real photoviews:	.75–$10 + according to subject

Advertising

Poster-ads (general):	$5–$25 according to subject
Product advertising & publicity:	$2.50–$15 + very wide range
Campbell Kids by Grace Wiederseim:	$25–$50
Coca-Cola (very scarce):	$200
Heinz:	$3–$15 for poster-ad type
Bensdorp Cocoa:	$2.50–$7.50 (wide range of sets)
Bell Telephone:	$7.50–$15 + for fire card
Singer Sewing Machines:	$2–$7.50
Footwear of Nations (Woonsocket Rubber Co.):	$5–$8
Kornelia Kinks:	$6–$10
Cracker Jack Bears:	$10–$20

Expositions (Official Issues only)

The issues of unofficial Expo cards were too many and varied to give any degree of accuracy to current market prices; much depends upon the publishers of such cards, eg Koehler issues for the World's Columbian, Chicago 1893 range from $18 to $25; Trans-Mississippi 1898 from $40 to $60; while the infinite choice of cards for subsequent expos in the unofficial class are priced at as little as $1 up to $30 plus.

World's Columbian, Chicago 1893—official publisher Charles W. Goldsmith: $12–$20

Trans-Mississippi 1898—official publisher Chicago Colortype Co.: $35–$60 +

Pan-American 1901—official publisher Niagara Envelope Manufactory: $7–$15

St Louis Purchase Expo 1904—official publisher Samuel Cupples:
  $8-$10
Lewis and Clark 1905—official publisher B. B. Rich (Portland): $4-$8
Jamestown 1907—official publisher Jamestown Amusement & Vending
  Co. Inc.: $3-$50
Alaska-Yukon 1909—official publisher Portland Post Card Co.,
  Oregon: $1—$3.50
Hudson-Fulton Celebrations (no official cards): $5-$15
Anglo-American Expo., London 1914—official publisher Gale &
  Polden: $2-$6
Panama-Pacific 1915—official publisher Cardinell-Vincent (San
  Francisco): $1.50-$7.50

Patriotic and Greetings Cards

Lincoln's Birthday:	from $3.50 up to $12 for the Rose 'Open Book' series
Lincoln's Centennial:	$5-$10
Washington's Birthday:	$2-$6
Memorial (Decoration) Day:	$3-$7
July 4 (Independence Day):	$4-$8
Uncle Sam cards:	$3-$15
Miss Liberty cards:	$2-$6
Thanksgiving:	.50-$4

Other Greetings

New Year's:	.35-$5 according to type
St. Valentine's:	$1-$4
St. Patrick's Day types:	.75-$4
Easter:	.35-$5 according to type
Labor Day (scarce):	$60-$100
April Fool's Day:	$4-$125 each for Lounsbury's set of 4
Ground Hog Day:	$5-$125 for Henderson Litho set of 4
Birthday:	.35-$2.50 according to type
Mother's Day:	$3-$10
Rally Day:	$1.50-$7
Hallowe'en:	$3.50-$35 for some Winsch designs
Christmas:	.35-$20+ for Santas

Novelty

Wood:	$3-$7.50
Aluminum (and other metals):	$3-$6
Celluloid (simulated ivory):	$4-$7.50

Leather:	$1–$3
Embroidered Silks WW1 (French):	$6–$9
Woven Silks (Steven's etc):	$25–$75
Huld Installment sets (composites):	$35–$100
H.T.L. Transparencies	$10–$35
H.T.L. cut-outs:	$20–$65 for Santas
Jig-saw and zag-saw puzzles:	$4–$8
Rebus:	$4–$8
Paper-doll and other toy novelties:	$30–$75
Squeakers:	$1–$6
Gramophone records (Tuck's):	$12–$16
Honeycomb double postcards:	$12–$17
Mechanical (kaleidoscope, roller blinds etc):	$12–$35

Appliqued cards using different materials such as real hair, fur, feathers, buttons, mother-of-pearl, shamrock seeds (in envelopes), metal charms, wire spring animal tails, velvets, silks, ginghams and cottons, and ribbon decoration were produced in too wide a variety to assess with any great accuracy, but the prices for such cards range from $1 to $25+.

Artist-Signed Postcards

American Girl series drawn by Charles Dana Gibson, Harrison Fisher, Howard Chandler Christy, F. Earl Christy, Philip Boileau, Archie Gunn, Clarence Underwood etc:		$7.50–$15
Sunbonnets	Bertha Corbett:	$6.50–$17.50
	Bernhardt Wall:	$8–$12.50
General	Frances Brundage:	$6–$25 for early Tuck's
	Ellen Clapsaddle:	$6–$15
	Katherine Gassaway:	$4–$6
	Grace Wiederseim:	$15–$25
	Rose O'Neill (Kewpies):	$22–$30
	Bessie Pease Gutmann:	$8–$10
	Bertha Blodgett:	$2–$5
	M. Greiner:	$3–$10
	Dwig:	$3.50–$20 for some Tuck designs
	Outcault (Buster Brown):	$3–$12.50
	Opper:	$4–$7
	Cobb X Shinn:	$1–$6
	Winsor McKay:	$5–$20

Elizabeth Curtis:	$2-$6
Florence Robinson:	$7.50-$10
Julia Woodworth (Cupids):	$4-$7
Catherine Klein:	$2-$5
Mary Golay:	$2-$5
Charles Russell:	$7-$15
Harry Payne:	$5-$12
Louis Wain:	$22-$35
Millicent Sowerby:	$5-$15
Pauli Ebner:	$8-$15
Florence Upton (Golliwogs):	$20-$25
Alice Luella Fidler:	$6-$9
Pearle Fidler Le Munyan:	$6-$9
The Kinneys:	$4-$7
Arthur Thiele:	$8-$20
H. Dix Sandford:	$10-$20
Samuel Schmucker:	$12.50 for Winsch to $50 for Detroits

Religion

Lord's Prayer (eight cards to a set):	$40-$80
Lord's Prayer published by P.F.B.:	$70-$90
Ten Commandments (ten to a set):	$70-$100
Virtues—Faith, Hope, Charity, etc:	$6-$9
Guardian Angels:	$5-$10
Jewish New Year:	$6-$10
Children's Prayer cards:	$5-$8
Hymn (and Song) cards:	$2.50-$5 depending upon publisher

Presidential and Political Cards

From the President McKinley mourning cards through the Presidential campaigns from 1900 to 1980, the list of postcard portraits, family groups, weddings, real photocards, Presidential Election campaign cards, cartoons etc, depicting Presidents Theodore Roosevelt, Taft, Wilson, Harding, Coolidge, Hoover, F.D.Roosevelt, Truman, Eisenhower, Kennedy, and Nixon are too plentiful and varied to list, but most of these cards come in the price range of $5 and $25 plus.

Suffragist cards
Wellman cartoons:	$6-$15
Rose O'Neill 'Kewpie' card:	$50-$75

Other cartoon types: $8–$15
Real photocards of suffragists, parades, demonstrations, etc: $5–$25

Prohibition
Cartoon types: $1–$10
Others: $1–$20

Ethnic

Indian Chiefs: $5–$9
Indian Reservations: $1–$5
Real photocards (Indian): $3.50–$15
Cartoon cards (Blacks): $4–$10
Cotton-picking: $1–$4
Cowboys: $1–$7.50

North Pole Exploration

Real photocards of Cook and Peary: $10–$15
Humor cards of Cook and Peary: $5–$10

Wartime Cards

Cards issued depicting specific wartime themes for the Spanish-American War and World Wars 1 and 2 are too numerous and varied to list and accurately assess from the price point of view, but certainly most of the cards in this category would be priced at $1 up to $15 plus.

Transportation

Trolley-cars—full close-up photographs: $6–$15
Steamers: $1–$5
Railroad stations: $1–$5
Railroad disasters: $3–$10
Automobiles—full close-up photographs: $3–$5
Automobile accidents: $3–$12.50
Early aviation—real photographs: $5–$15
Aviators: $3–$15
Aviation meets: $6–$15
Aviation disasters: $5–$15
Shipping cards (liners): $2–$5
Shipping wrecks: $3–$10

Miscellaneous

Cinema Stars: $1–$10 for Shirley Temple, Charlie Chaplin etc

Early Theater Stars: $1–$5
Disney cards: $8–$12
Space Travel (modern): .50–$1.50

BIBLIOGRAPHY

American Postcard Guide to Tuck, Sally S. Carver, Chestnut Hill, Massachusetts—first published 1976. Now into its 3rd printing with updated prices as of May 1980

Collecting Postcards in Colour 1894-1914, William Dûval with Valerie Monahan, Blandford Press, Poole, Dorset, UK 1978

Collecting Postcards in Colour 1914-1930, Valerie Monahan, Blandford Press, Poole, Dorset, UK 1980

Picture Postcards of the Golden Age, Tonie and Valmai Holt, MacGibbon & Kee, UK 1971

A Directory of Postcards, Artists, Publishers and Trademarks, Barbara Andrews, Little Red Caboose 1975—excellent book for all deltiologists

Fantasy Postcards, William Ouellette and Barbara Jones, Sphere Books 1975

Mail Memories: Pictorial Guide to Postcard Collecting, John Kaduck, Des Moines, Iowa, USA, 1971—revised 1975

Patriotic Postcards, John Kaduck, Des Moines, Iowa, USA 1974

Rare and Expensive Postcards, John Kaduck, Des Moines, Iowa, USA 1975

Transportation Postcards, John Kaduck, Des Moines, Iowa, USA 1976

Picture Postcards in the United States 1893-1918, George and Dorothy Miller, published Clarkson N. Potter, Inc/Publisher, New York, distributed by Crown Publishers Inc. 1976. Highly recommended

Pioneer Postcards, Jefferson Burdick, Voss Litho 1957—reprinted by Nostalgia Press

The Artist Signed Postcard, Forrest D. Lyons, Gas City, Indiana 1975

The Picture Postcard and its Origins, Frank Staff, Lutterworth Press, UK 1966—reprint 1979

Picture Postcards and Travel, Frank Staff, Lutterworth Press, UK 1979

Picture Postcards and Their Publishers, Anthony Byatt, Golden Age Postcard Books, Malvern, Worcs., UK 1978

Checklist Books

Postcards for Pleasure, published and edited by Tony Warr and Ken Lawson—series 1 *Tom Browne*, published 1978; series 2 *Lance Thackeray* published 1979. MCC/SPA, Wembley, UK

Jessie Wilcox Smith, S. M. Schnessel, published by Thomas Crowell, New York, USA

Paul Finkenrath, Berlin (PFB), Edward McAllister, published USA

Rose O'Neill, Janet Banneck, checklist published USA

Detroit Publishing Company Collectors' Guide, Lowe and Papell, published USA

Ellen H. Clapsaddle, Elisabeth K. Austin, privately printed 1967, Pawcatuck, Connecticut

INDEX

Figures in **bold** refer to color illustrations.